D1346322

Dean's Grange Cemetery

Stories From Beyond The Grave

Dean's Grange Cemetery

Stories From Beyond The Grave

JAMIE MORAN

Chuil Aoibhinn Publications

Published 2009 by Chuil Aoibhinn Publications

Jamie Moran
jmoranjnr5@eircom.net

ISBN 978-0-9561729-0-7

Printed and bound in the UK by J F Print Ltd, Sparkford, Somerset

Contents

Photo Credits

Peter Graham, courtesy of Independent News & Media and Irish Newspaper Archives Ltd.

Francis Saunders, from " Lifeboats in Dublin Bay" 1997, John de Courcy Ireland. Courtesy of Stephen Wynne & RNLI

Francis Browning from "The Pals at Suvla Bay" 1917, Henry Hanna. Courtesy of Sean Connolly, Royal Dublin Fusiliers Association.

J Blissett, Montague Browne, Frederick Dietrichsen, courtesy of the WFR Museum (Sherwood Foresters Collection) & Maj J O M Hackett (Retd)

Charles 'Leo' Murphy, courtesy of Brendan Costello.

Thomas Murphy, courtesy of Thomas Callaghan, Thomas Kelly, Pauline Keegan & Bernard Kelly.

Joseph Hudson, courtesy of the Hudson family.

Reginald Dunne & Joseph O'Sullivan, Mass cards courtesy of Sean O'Mahony

James 'Jimmy' Dunne, collectors card.

Philip Francis Little, courtesy of Bert Riggs, Memorial University of Newfoundland.

Davy Stephens, postcard.

Joseph Edward Woodall, I don't remember where I came across this picture. I would appeal to anyone who does know to contact me.

William Maher, Frances 'Fanny' Saunders, Sinking of RMS Leinster, Capt Robert Lee & Elizabeth Ellam, all courtesy of Philip Lecane.

Solway Disaster, Supplement to the Illustrated London News December 3 1881.

Robert Kinston Gray, courtesy of Colin Scudds & Dún Laoghaire Borough Historical Society, Journal 9.

Old picture Dean's Grange Cemetery, courtesy of Nicola Jennings.

All other photos in this publication are from my own personal collection.

Dedicated to my brother Martin
and to all those buried in the Angels Plot.

"An angel came to say hello but never got to speak,
the breath he had for so long waited was not there to greet.

A mother only knows the pain, the regrets at not been able
to see your face or kiss your lips or hold you in her embrace.

Although you never got to meet you are always in her thoughts,
you sleep forever knowing that one day you will be in her arms"

Acknowledgments

Due to various reasons it has taken me a long time to complete this book and many people have helped and gave encouragement to me over those years. None more so than my parents James & Anita, who without their support and guidance I would never have finished this book or even started writing for that matter. My fiancée Tina who was also of immense support and encouragement and I thank them all for their help and patience.

I would like to express my deepest gratitude to Sean O'Mahony for editing this book, his advice and our good chats. I would especially like to thank the staff in Dean's Grange Cemetery, Ann Kinsella, Bernie Murphy, Eavan Henderson and Aoife Flynn for all their help over the years and for putting up with my intrusions into their work schedules. Eugene Vesey for his advice when I had lost direction. Thomas Kelly, Thomas Callaghan, Pauline Keegan, Bernard Kelly, Brendan Costello and Jason McLean niece and nephews of Republican Volunteers and also the Hudson family. I you like to thank the Dún Laoghaire Genealogical Society for the kind use of their publications Memorial Inscriptions of Dean's Grange Cemetery Volumes 1 to 5. Neil Fetherston and Ken Finlay of the Southside People. Philip Lecane (Torpedoed! / The RMS Leinster Disaster) for his help and advice.

Others gave assistance, advice, and information for which I am grateful and for which I thank each of them. Vicky Cremin, the late Dr John de Courcy Ireland, Liam O'Donovan, Olive Mannion, Bert Riggs (Newfoundland), Ian Hearn, (Wexford), Martin Allen (DLRCC), Roy Stokes, Stephen Wynne and the RNLI, Stephen Hughes (OPW), Nicola Jennings. Colin Scudds and the Dún Laoghaire Borough Heritage Society. Rosaleen Dunphy (DLRCC), Michael Nolan for his work on the cemetery map.

If, for any reason, I may have forgotten to include some people, my deepest apologies. This book was a long time in the making and it was not always possible to keep notes about those to whom I spoke over the years.

Introduction

As a young boy growing up in Dún Laoghaire. I was regularly taken by my mother to visit the graves of my grandparents in Dean's Grange Cemetery. I didn't really see it at the time as a cemetery, but more as a place of adventure, playing hide-and-seek with my cousin Tony, or jumping from grave to grave while trying not to stand on the clay. I never gave much attention to the thousands of other graves and the people buried within them, who they were or where they were from. Only two graves in the whole cemetery were all I ever thought of.

That all changed in the summer of 1996 when I got my first permanent job working with Dún Laoghaire-Rathdown County Council and I was posted to Dean's Grange Cemetery. I remember starting and not really having a clue what I was in for as I didn't think graves were still dug by hand. I was shaking with fear when I had to carry the coffin during my first funeral and digging the graves by hand was a physically demanding job. At the start I didn't think I would be able to continue working in the grounds but one of the more experienced men told me it would get easier and that I should stick it out.

As the months passed, the job did get better and I settled into the surroundings of the cemetery. Over the months my instinctive interest in history drew me towards names on the different headstones as I went about my work each day and I soon began to learn of the people buried here. The headstones particularly in the older wooded sections appealed to me and I found some of the inscriptions very interesting.

I decided I wanted to find out how these diverse people had died and, in turn, to write about their deaths and lives. At the start of my research I came across a publication which was written by local historian Vicky Cremin. This gave me a starting point but I wanted to write more in-depth pieces linking those buried here with the main events of our history. I not only wanted to list each of these people but I also wanted to show their human side. Where I can I have given their age, last place of residence, family and depending on the individual a brief look at their life. I have also attempted to show how they died and where in the cemetery they are buried as well as a description of the memorial.

Throughout the book you will come across the names Kingstown and Dún Laoghaire. Confusingly the present day town of Dún Laoghaire was named Kingstown between 1821 and 1920. It was then proposed in July 1920 to rename the town back to its proper title of Dún Laoghaire. Both town names have been in use during the cemetery's history but I have chosen only to use Dún Laoghaire when referring to the area throughout that time. The name Kingstown still appears but only where it is quoted in a memorial inscription or similar.

Cemetery Overview

> *'Graveyards are not to be feared, as the dead can do you no harm. Tread lightly in the tranquility and stillness of its grounds and let those beneath sleep sound.'*

The following pages provide a general overview of Dean's Grange Cemetery, why there was a need for it to be constructed and a look at its history. The chapter covers changes in the cemetery's administration up until the present day and some interesting facts about the day to day goings-on inside its walls.

Dún Laoghaire (Kingstown) and the surrounding townships witnessed many changes in the first half of the nineteenth century. Two major projects were undertaken, that of the construction of the harbour and the introduction of the Dublin to Dún Laoghaire railway. The harbour had become the most prominent port in Ireland, which was further boosted by its rail link with Dublin city. The construction of the two projects offered the local population the possibility of work and a better life, but also brought many more families to the area in search of employment.

By the middle of the nineteenth century, graveyards and burial grounds throughout Ireland were becoming overcrowded. This was in the main part due to the starving to death of over a million people during the Famine when a potato blight caused the failure of the crop in the 1840s. Rural areas were hardest hit by the Famine and this in turn forced many families to seek help in the larger towns and cities and in many cases other countries. The difficulties in Dún Laoghaire worsened further at the start of the 1860s, when the local graveyard in Dalkey was closed aalong with the news that burials in the Kill O' the Grange graveyard would have to cease within a short number of years. Initially Kill O' the Grange graveyard was to be closed straight away but due to local opposition it was permitted to continue until such time as a new cemetery was completed and operational.

Following the introduction of the Burial Ground (Ireland) Act in 1856, the Board of Guardians of the Rathdown Poor Law Union was constituted a Burial Board. It was also empowered to purchase land for the construction and maintenance of a new cemetery for the south-east of Dublin. The Union operated under the 'Poor Law Act' from the Loughlinstown Workhouse, which is now St Columcille's Hospital and administered a degrading form of Victorian social welfare for those that were unable to take care of themselves.

In November 1861, the Rathdown Union purchased the first land for this new cemetery beside the small village of Dean's Grange, roughly two kilometres west of the town of Dún Laoghaire. The original land, which measured about eight acres, was sold to the Rathdown Union by the owner, the Rev John Beatty, for the amount of £200 which was based on a lump sum of 20 years rent which the Rev Beatty had himself requested. Today, this original eight acre site covers the lower North and South sections to a point just beyond and in line with the two Chapels.

A standing committee to oversee the running of the cemetery was formed, consisting of Guardians of the Rural Districts of the Union and on Wednesday, the 20th of November 1861, the Union Chairman; Sir George Hobson signed the deeds, which officially saw the beginning of the Dean's Grange Cemetery.

The Cemetery Committee appointed a man by the name of Matthew Betham as Chairman. An office clerk named Joseph D. Cope was also appointed and he would oversee the day-to-day administration duties of the new burial ground. Cope was also the clerk for the Rathdown Union

An old photograph of Dean's Grange Cemetery with the Gate Lodge in the background

and his responsibilities were extended to take in the building of the new burial ground. Incidentally, Joseph Cope died in 1899 and was interred in a vault which sits at the top left hand side of the main walkway. You will notice a carved marble profile of Cope to the front of his vault and to the bottom left, you can see the vault's stone entrance.

It was decided by the Committee in May 1862 that the laying out of the new cemetery should include separate sections for both Catholic and Protestant religions. They also decided that a Registrar's house should be built at the main gate and from there a spacious main walkway would run towards two chapels that would be built at the far end of each of the new sections. The grounds were planned in an ornamental design. Yew trees were planted along each side of the main walkway and along two smaller pathways leading to the chapels.

In May 1862, the committee applied for and received a loan of £5,000 from the Lord Lieutenant of Ireland to cover the construction of the buildings, external walls, paths, as well as ground drainage and landscaping. This government loan was to be repaid by the Board of Guardians of the Rathdown Union through the raising of local rates, much to the disappointment of local traders and land owners.

Work commenced the following year on the drainage of the eight acre site so as to have the soil as dry as possible for the laying of foundations and grave digging. The construction of the outer walls and internal pathways had also begun. By the end of June that year the Rathdown Union placed advertisements in local newspapers inviting builders to submit tenders for the construction of the Gate Lodge (Registrar's House) and the two chapels. It was decided that contractors by the name of Matthew Gahan & Son would be offered the contract as they submitted the cheapest quote. Matthew Gahan had tendered a costing of £1,305 to complete the entire work, which he calculated as follows:

Protestant Chapel	£390.8s
Catholic Chapel	£397.6s
Gate Lodge	£517

The Gate Lodge was the living quarters of the Registrar right up until the late 1990s, when the last incumbent finally vacated his post. Dún Laoghaire-Rathdown County Council took over from the Burial Board in January 1994 and there would no longer be a need for a Registrar. The Lodge also doubled as the cemetery office before the office used today was built and from here the Registrar would oversee the administration and running of the cemetery and would meet bereaved relatives who arrived to choose a burial plot for their deceased loved ones.

As the cemetery grew in size and the number of burials increased, the decision was taken in 1898 to build an office and public toilets opposite the lodge. Up to this point the staff were finding it increasingly cumbersome to work in the house as the lodge also doubled as the Registrar's family home. Plans were drawn up and the present offices were constructed just inside the main gate. Today these offices hold

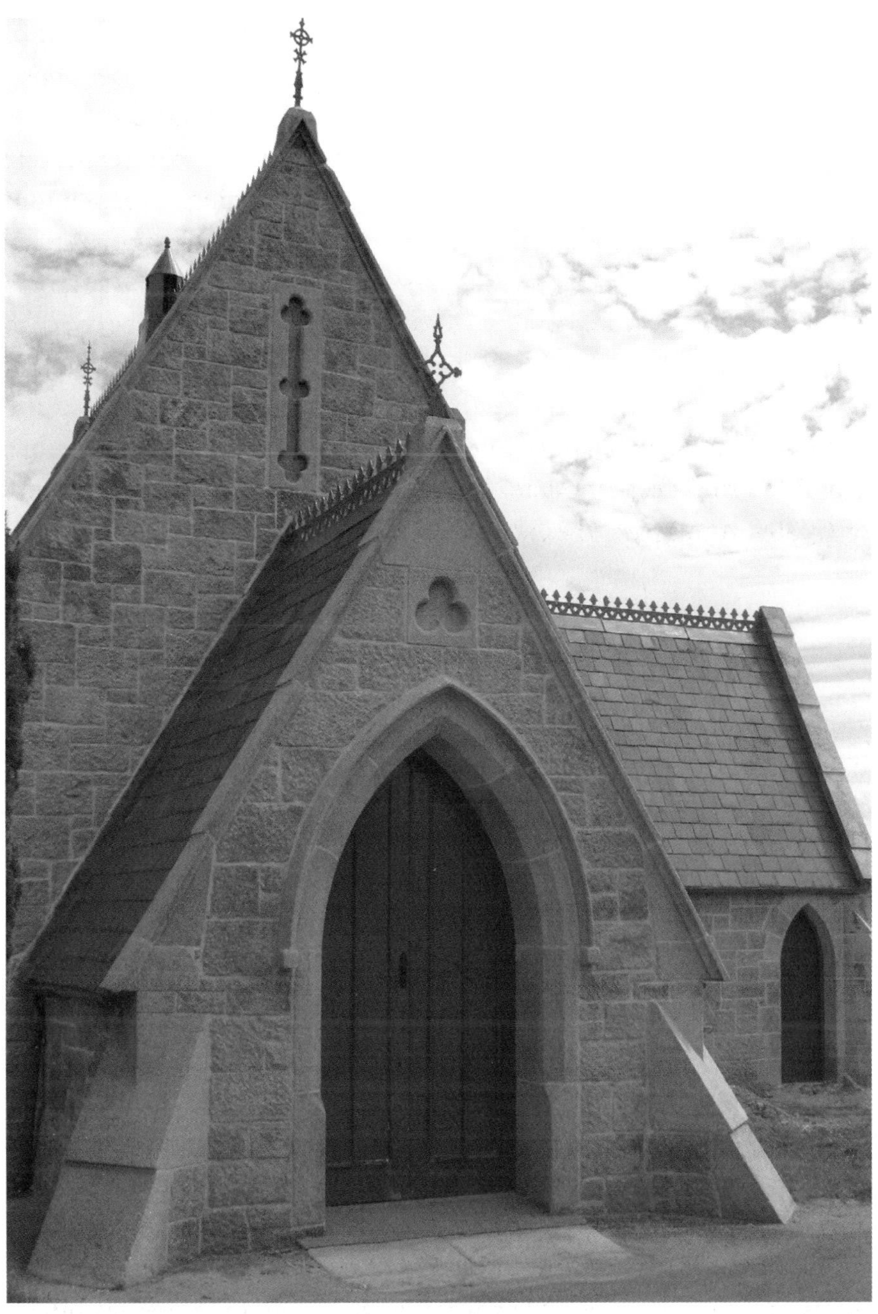

Protestant chapel

the large books containing Registry of Interment records, which date back to that of the first burial in 1865. The books record the burial information of each individual interred within the cemetery, and list the person's name, age, religion, occupation, marital status, address, date of death, date of burial and plot number. In many cases the signature of a family member can also be found here as they signed their permission for the burial. Other records list the sections and plots in alphabetical order and how many people are buried within each one. Also the depth of each coffin is recorded so that the grave digger will know how far to dig down when the grave is next opened and also how many burials will be allowed into the grave. Even now these books are used on a daily basis by the office staff, who have to take the utmost care when handling them. Many of the older books are made from pig skin and special care is required when handling them. Nowadays the record books are made of a synthetic skin.

The lodge and chapels were completed in time for the cemetery's opening in 1865. All three buildings were constructed to a very high standard using Killiney granite and can still be seen in near perfect condition. The two chapels were recently brought under the control of An Taisce. Restoration works on the outer walls and roofs have been completed and for the first time both chapels now have electricity. There is a sloped pathway leading to the rear of each building where a metal doorway opens up into the vaults beneath. The title, 'Matthew. Gahan &. Son 1864' can clearly be seen marked on each of these metal doors. There are seven vaults under each chapel but only a small number of these were ever purchased and used. William Burnell, who was one of the cemetery's first Registrars and founder of the Burnell Monumental Works, is interred in a vault under the Protestant chapel.

The two chapels were designed so that each was facing in a westerly direction. Even today when burials are performed in Dean's Grange the coffin is lowered so that it faces east, (feet east – head west). Because many of the grave plots in the cemetery lie in sporadic directions the coffins are placed as near to facing east as possible.

I have been told a number of different explanations for this, one that as the chapel altars face west, so those buried around them should face the altar or priest. Another reason is that those buried will always face the rising sun, but in a way both explanations are correct. The decision to have burials undertaken in this manner was a common practice in burial grounds, as Christians believe that the resurrection of the Son of God will rise from the East and those deceased shall be ready to face him on that judgment day.

> *'For as lighting cometh out of the east and appeareth even into the west, so shall also the coming of the son of man be.'*
>
> Matthew 24:27

One day, after a funeral had just ended in Dean's Grange Cemetery, the chief mourner approached one of the grave diggers. This man seemed confused as to why his mother's coffin had just been lowered into the grave with her feet under the headstone, which he thought was the wrong way round. The grave digger explained the reason behind this and the man asked if his father, who died a number of years earlier, was buried in the same way. He was told that his father was buried that way and with this the man burst into roars of laughter, stooped over with both hands on his knees. After a few moments the man composed himself, looked up at the grave digger with tears in his eyes, put a hand on his shoulder and said with a big smile:

'I'm sorry! I've just realised that my mother was kneeling there every Sunday for the past twelve years, talking to my father's feet!'

Such a positive outlook on such a sad day...

In January 1865, the Board of Guardians placed an advertisement in local newspapers with different grave prices for the poor and wealthy. The advert informed the public of the opening of Dean's Grange Cemetery and the cost of burials. The decision was taken to open the cemetery that January with immediate effect, as the nearby Kill O' the

Grange graveyard was due to be closed by March, resulting in the need for grave spaces. On the 28th of January 1865, the first of many funeral processions passed through the main gates when Anastasia Carey was laid to rest in a grave close to the Catholic Chapel. (See Chapter on Notable People)

There were basically four grave types that could be chosen by bereaved families. These could be either purchased or rented and were classed as follows.

1st Class graves were those adjacent to the main pathways and considered the most prominent in the cemetery. Only wealthy families could afford these graves and many of the headstones on the main walkway show just how wealthy they were.

2nd Class graves were those directly adjacent to the smaller pathways, so that anyone visiting the plot did not have to cross another grave in order to pay their respects. Again these plots were bought by those who could afford them and almost all of them have headstones.

3rd Class graves are surrounded on all sides by other plots. These graves were also allowed to be purchased within a five year period but failure to do so could result in the grave falling back under the control of the Burial Board and could be reused.

4th Class graves were merely on loan and used to bury those whose family could not afford it. After a number of years the grave would fall back under the control of the Burial Board and be reused. Evidence of this is clearly noticeable behind the office in the South section, where a number of modern headstones appear among the older ones as the graves were sold later on.

This 'loan' of graves was a common dilemma for many Catholic families and to a lesser extent some Protestants who could not afford to purchase the plots. If the families were not in a position to come up with the purchase fee, then the grave would be sold to some other family. This is very evident when one looks at the number of headstones in the South and South-West sections compared to those in the North and West, which are the old Catholic sections. A grave with no headstone does not automatically mean that it was not purchased, but is more likely to be due to the inability of families to pay for a memorial. In some cases families resorted to planting trees on the graves as a substitute headstone and rows of the trees can still be spotted in some areas where they were allowed to continue to grow. These are mainly from the cypress conifer family, western red cedar and the Lawson cypress being the most popular trees used. These tall, narrow trees are commonly found in groups around the older sections and make up the vast majority of the wooded areas. Their cousin the Monterey cypress is a much larger conifer and because of its size tends to be more isolated. Its branches are broader and it can be found in the West and upper North sections and to the far right hand corner of the South-West. Many of the trees in the cemetery have caused damage to memorials over the years. In 2008 a program of removing dangerous trees was undertaken, which will result in scores of these trees being felled.

Trees have played an important role within burial grounds through the centuries. This is clearly evident with the use of yew trees. There was a spiritual reason for the planting of yew trees in burial grounds for many years and it is still very common to see yews growing in old and new graveyards around the country. The yew has a very long life span, with some varieties believed to be over 2,000 years old, and this is thought to be one of the reasons for its use in burial grounds. This longevity had a spiritual significance for many pagans and ultimately Christians, which over the centuries led them to bury their dead near the trees roots. There are two varieties of this tree planted around the old sections of Dean's Grange Cemetery. The trees you see along the pathways are the Irish yew. These were planted in lines along the pathways and are tied around the sides with wire and clipped in order to keep their neat appearance. The common yews are not as noticeable as the Irish yews, but can be found in the centre of the lower North and South sections. Here the large, broad-leafed common yews stand surrounded by the taller cypress conifers. Their size gives an impression that they are aged trees, but it is unclear whether these trees were planted before the cemetery was constructed in 1862. There are also various other plants and trees growing in and around the wooded areas and together these really add to the overall character and beauty of the cemetery's landscape.

Passing through the main gates into Dean's Grange Cemetery, you enter an area surrounded by the grandeur of gothic memorials that this burial ground has to offer. This immediate area is within the older section of the graveyard, with the Gate Lodge on the right and the offices and public toilets to the left. Leading up through the cemetery in front of you is the main tree-lined walkway; which separates the old Protestant and Catholic sections of the South and lower North respectively. The monuments that face each other from opposite sides of the main walkway symbolise the architecture consistent with memorials from the nineteenth century and are some of the most impressive within the grounds. There are many different types of headstones throughout the cemetery and all tell a different story.

Tablet – the most common form of headstone in Dean's Grange Cemetery. The monuments are mainly rectangular, upright, and flat and can be made from marble, granite, sandstone or slate. Styles can also differ with 'dome' and 'shoulder' forms cut out of the top of the stone and some also have the additional feature of a cross.

Latin cross – these are also referred to as the Christian cross and are plain in design. They are mainly situated in the Catholic sections of the cemetery and represent the cross on which Jesus was crucified.

Calvary cross – this is similar to the Latin cross but the difference is that these rest on three tiered plinths. The tiers which lead up to the cross are said to represent the hill of Calvary or are a symbol of Faith, Hope and Love.

Celtic cross – these are abundant in all sections of the cemetery with sizes reaching heights of up to 20 feet or more. This Celtic style dates back to the fifth century and consists of a cross and circle which symbolises eternity. The crosses are regularly found to be decorated with Celtic knots and elaborate engravings, which are interwoven and placed in sections around the entire monument.

Pedestal – these are usually monuments made from one large piece of stone which is then carved with ornate designs on all four sides. Some have the added extra of an urn at the summit which indicates someone who was lost or cremated. The styles originate from the old Roman and Greek periods.

Broken Columns & Angels – these indicate that the person buried there has died young. Not necessarily the death of a child but someone cut down in the prime of their life.

Ledgers & Scrolls - are exactly as the names state. Ledgers are usually a depiction of an open bible, referring to the word of God. Some will have the name of those deceased on each page, where others will have a passage from the bible engraved on one side and name on the opposite. Scrolls are carvings which symbolise ancient manuscripts which are rolled at each end. The inscription is etched on the flat face of the monument.

Some of the memorials positioned off the main walkway and pathways towards the chapels have a unique design as they appear to resemble church spires. They have an **Eclectic** design, which may indicate a family burial plots of local craftsmen and builders and in some cases members of the clergy.

If you need to find a grave, check the back of a headstone nearby. Many of the headstones throughout the cemetery have their plot number etched on the back for reference.

There is one very important plot located at the top of the North section, that of the Angels' Plot. This plot was used to bury the remains of children from 1905 right up until 1989. No actual record was kept for this plot, but it is believed that as many as 750 angels were buried here over that time. Recently the Angels' Plot was renovated by cemetery staff and it now stands as a fitting memorial to those buried there.

Over the past 143 years, responsibility for Dean's Grange Cemetery has shifted as different governmental Acts were introduced over that period. When the Public Health (Ireland) Act was introduced in 1878, the Board of Guardians of the Rathdown Union became the sole Burial Board for the rural area of Rathdown. The Urban District Councils of Dún Laoghaire, Dalkey and Blackrock were prohibited from having Burial Boards for their own areas and so the responsibility was passed to the Board of Guardians. The town lands of Ballybrack and Killiney became a combined Urban Sanitary District, by provisional order under the same Act. This also carried with it the responsibility for burials in that area but the new District discharged its duty under the Act and contributed to the management of Dean's Grange Cemetery.

Responsibility for the cemetery shifted again when the 1898 Local Government (Ireland) Act saw the administration transferred from the Board of Guardians to the combined control of the four Urban District Councils (Blackrock, Dún Laoghaire, Dalkey, & Killiney / Ballybrack) and the Rathdown No.1 Rural District Council.

By provisional order under the 1878 Act, dated the 30th of May 1899, the five Councils were declared a United District for the purpose of managing Dean's Grange Cemetery, with the new governing body becoming the Dean's Grange Joint Burial Board. The Board membership consisted of the Chairman of each of the District Councils and ex-officio members as well as 14 elected members as follows:

Blackrock UDC	3 Members
Kingstown (Dún Laoghaire) UDC	5 Members
Dalkey UDC	1 Member
Killiney / Ballybrack UDC	1 Member
Rathdown No.1 RDC	4 Members

The cost of running the cemetery was funded from a joint account contributed to by each District, based on the poor law valuation in their areas.

Although responsibility for the Burial Board shifted between alternating Acts, the Board ultimately came under the control of the government. The cemetery would see the changing of government Acts lead to the changing of governments.

At a meeting of the Joint Burial Board on the 9th of December 1921 a motion was passed by the members, to the effect that they would refuse to allow the British Local Government to have any access to the cemetery records.

> '. . . *the members of the Dean's Grange Joint Burial Board hereby pledge our allegiance to An Dail Eireann and that all minutes of future meetings of the Board be submitted to the Minister for Local Government of An Dail . . .*'
> '*That the Registrar of the Dean's Grange Joint Burial Board be hereby directed to refuse to allow the Auditor of the British Local Government to audit any of the books in the keeping of the Registrar.*'

This decision taken by the Burial Board was not an isolated one as the same motion was passed by government-run agencies throughout the country as they pledged their allegiances to Dail Éireann when the Treaty settlement was negotiated.

In 1930, Saorstát Éireann (Irish Free State) introduced their own amendments regarding local authorities through the Local Government (Dublin) Act. Under this Act the four local Urban Districts Councils were dissolved and amalgamated under the new single authority to be known as the Corporation of Dún Laoghaire. The Rural District Council of Rathdown No.1 was also dissolved and its powers were transferred to the Dublin Board of Public Health. In 1940, the powers of the D.B.P.H. were reassigned to the control of Dublin County Council.

Dean's Grange Cemetery was reconstituted, and the new Joint Burial Board was now made up of 16 member's comprising the Chairmen of the Dún Laoghaire Corporation and Dublin City Council, as well as 14 elected members from: (Dún Laoghaire x 10 / Dublin CoCo x 4)

In 1984, the Dean's Grange Joint Burial Board opened its new sister cemetery just south of the village of Shankill. The new cemetery covers roughly 50 acres and was named Shanganagh because of it proximity to Shanganagh Castle and lands.

In 1994, the districts of the Corporation of Dún Laoghaire, the Dean's Grange Joint Burial Board and a section of south-east Dublin County Council were amalgamated to form the County of Dún Laoghaire-Rathdown. Presently the cemetery is administered by Dún Laoghaire-Rathdown County Council through its sub-department of Culture, Community Development & Amenities, which oversees the running of Dean's Grange and Shanganagh Cemeteries as well as the closed burial grounds.

Burials are still carried out in Dean's Grange Cemetery six days a week. The amount of burials per day fluctuates from no burials at all up to as many as ten or more. The graves spaces in this old cemetery were not designed to facilitate mechanical diggers, so many of the graves are still dug by hand. The job carried out by the gravediggers is a tough one. both mentally and physically. Apart from maintenance and carrying out burials, graves have to be dug within a short time frame and could be to a depth of eight feet. This is no problem if the work can be reached by a mechanical digger but otherwise pure human strength using a pick and shovel is required. Over 142,000 burials have taken place in Dean's Grange Cemetery since it opened in 1864 and the vast majority of these were dug by hand. Of the 16 sections which make up this cemetery, South, South-West, North, and West are in the older wooded area. The remaining 12 sections are all named after Saints and have been in operation since the 1930s when St Patrick's section was opened. Presently the cemetery covers an area of over 70 acres, which makes it the second largest cemetery in the country, but since the late 1980s the selling of new grave spaces has had to cease due to the unavailability of land.

Dean's Grange, for many years to come, will operate as the largest cemetery in the County of Dún Laoghaire-Rathdown. It is far removed from becoming a closed burial ground and, in fact, many changes and refurbishments are proposed for the near future. The history of this cemetery and its links to local families has for many years made it a much sought after 'final resting place'. Included in the proposed refurbishments is the allocation of a small number of new grave spaces as previously unused land is developed for burials.

I would like to acknowledge the lovely Sally, who for many years has sold flowers to people visiting the cemetery. Through good times and bad,Sally and her family have ensured that flowers have always been available to those who come to pay their respects.

Sea Disasters

'The rage of the storm and the gust of the gale,
the swell and the wave against the sail.
A ship in such waters is a tragedy of the sea.'

Many of the headstones in Dean's Grange Cemetery bear witness to the countless tragedies that have occurred in the surrounding waters off Dún Laoghaire. Like any port throughout the world, the connection between its people and the sea is part of their culture, their ability to live and prosper and, of course, death due to the tragedies they regularly have to face.

Anyone who takes a stroll through the older sections of Dean's Grange will see many headstones engraved with anchors and ships or inscriptions dedicated to captains, sailors, and coxswains. The reality of sea disasters is that most of those who are lost are never recovered and the sea becomes their grave forever.

Three of the tragedies that occurred in the waters stand out for the sheer calamitous nature of the events and their subsequent connection with Dean's Grange Cemetery. It was the ferocity of nature, along with human fallibility, that led to the loss of lives in the first of these tragedies. The sea itself did not take their lives but the combination of wind, water, and human error ultimately did on the 16th of November 1881.

The Steam Ship 'Solway'

The *Solway* was a brand new steam ship weighing 700 tons and transporting mainly cargo. She was manned by a crew of 20 and was carrying another 14 passengers. The *Solway* was bound from Glasgow to Bristol with its cargo of oils, whiskey, rum, sugar, seeds and other goods. She docked at Belfast port on her way from Glasgow on the morning of the 15th of November and sailed on from there later that afternoon.

As the ship left Belfast harbour it ran straight into a storm but the captain, Mr Fry, decided that they should continue on their voyage. At about 5:45 the following morning the captain was notified that the ship's rudder chain had become entangled in the engine gear and that the *Solway* was uncontrollable. The ship was now rolling violently from side to side as the crew tried in vain to release the rudder. As the *Solway* was tossed around in the rough sea, a number of barrels of naphtha oil came loose from their lashings and burst open upon the forward main deck. The oil quickly mixed with the sea water, which then flowed along the passageways on either side of the ship towards the steerage cabin.

Within the steerage cabin, a number of the passengers were crowded around a small potbelly stove, trying to keep warm. At the same time the flammable oil washed down into the cabin and came into contact with the fire causing an explosion that engulfed the entire room in flames.

Everyone within the cabin was immediately overcome by the blaze and all but one man were unable to escape the inferno. Some of the lucky few who managed to make it to the door fell in the narrow passageways and were also engulfed by the flames. The remainder of the crew escaped the blaze to the relative safety of the ship's stern, but some of them suffered severe burns. The whole scene was described as one of panic and horror; witnesses recalled how they could hear the desperate cries from those caught in the cabin before their screams eventually died out.

Sifting for remains after the Solway disaster

Fearing that the fire would reach the rest of the ship, five of those on board launched a small boat over the side and clambered aboard, preferring to take their chances with the raging sea against those of the burning *Solway*. The five sailed off towards land but were all later reported missing, presumed drowned.

The captain of the *Solway*, William Fry, ordered the crew to throw buckets of water on the fire and, with the aid of a donkey engine pump, they were able to hose it down, successfully preventing the fire from spreading any further.

It was not until between 5 and 6 o'clock in the evening on the 16th that help finally arrived when a pilot boat spotted the distress signals coming from the *Solway*. The pilot boat was able to steer the *Solway* towards the harbour of Dún Laoghaire (Kingstown).

The survivors were taken ashore on the *Solway*'s arrival at the quay side at Dún Laoghaire, and those with burns were conveyed to the nearby St Michael's Hospital. The local police and coastguard boarded the ship and were horrified at what they found. The main mast and main deck were totally gutted. In the steerage cabin, lay the remains of six badly charred bodies. It was reported that their clothes and flesh were so completely burned that their bones could be clearly seen. It was believed that there were another six bodies, so badly burned that the authorities had to sieve through the ashes in order to find their few remains.

One of the ship's passengers, Charles Byrne was brought to St Michael's Hospital with severe burns. He was fully conscious and aware of what had happened on board the ship and gave details of his identity. Unfortunately Charles was unable to fight off the effects of the fire and succumbed to his injuries the following day.

Charles Byrne was a 25 year old sailor from Swansea in Wales and had left behind a wife and young child. He was the only passenger to escape from the steerage when the fire first broke out. His remains were interred along with the other victims in the lower North section of Dean's Grange Cemetery. Two of the graves contain coffins, each holding the remains of three of the victims. The remaining six people were buried in separate graves; all eight plots are within the same area of the lower North.

Not all the names of the victims were known, but the *Irish Times* newspaper reported that five of them were soldiers of the 24th and

56th regiments. Two of the soldiers were transporting a deserter whom they had in their custody. Their names are Cpl Keeffe, Pte Quigley and Pte Campbell of the 24th. Keeffe was not buried in Dean's Grange. Charles Devine, Andrew Christy and a man named Rease all of whom were from Swansea, as well as an elderly lady named Ellen McKenzie and a teenage boy were also among the victims.

In July 1887 a woman by the name of Eliza Parkinson purchased a grave in Dean's Grange which contained the remains of three of those who perished on the *Solway*. As the remains could not be identified, Mrs Parkinson believed that her husband, George Parkinson, a passenger on board the ship, was one of those buried here. Eliza made arrangements to have a headstone dedicated to George, placed on the grave. This act in some way must have eased the hardship she suffered at the loss of her husband.

The memorial to George Parkinson is situated at plot number 93 K in the centre of the lower North. There is a small limestone cross on the grave which is now overgrown by brambles and holly. The following words are inscribed on the plinth underneath:

'In loving memory of George Henry Parkinson,
beloved husband of Eliza Parkinson.
He perished by the burning of the SS Solway
November 16th 1881, Age 32 Years.'
'To be with Christ which is far better.'

Palme / RNLI Disaster

The greatest single tragedy to be thrust on the Royal National Lifeboat Institution and the local people of Dún Laoghaire occurred on Christmas Eve 1895, when 15 local men of the volunteer Lifeboat Station lost their lives while answering the call of duty to a ship in distress.

For that entire Christmas week in 1895, the Irish coast was battered by a furious south-westerly gale. All lifeboat crews along the Irish coast were on standby or in action as ships sought shelter from the continuing storm. At around 11.30 on the morning of the 24th of December, the crews of the Dún Laoghaire Lifeboat Station were observing a ship in distress just outside the harbour mouth. The *Palme*, a 997 ton Russian barge bound from Liverpool to South America, was attempting to enter the safety of the harbour without success. The *Palme* which set sail on the 18th of December had called first into Belfast Port on her voyage down the Irish Sea. When the ship sailed as far as the coast off Dún Laoghaire, her captain endeavoured to reach the safety of the harbour in order to avoid the storm. While the ship was attempting to navigate the harbour entrance the gale swept her past the mouth and grounded her in the shallow waters of Merrion Strand to the north-west of the harbour.

By this time, the Dún Laoghaire lifeboat (Civil Service No. 7) with its 15 crewmen aboard put to sea in a rescue bid. The lifeboat sailed out of the harbour to within a mile of the *Palme* where her sails were lowered and the crew took to the oars. The strength and courage of these men was amazing as they rowed through the storm toward the stricken ship. As it was nearing the *Palme* the lifeboat suddenly disappeared in a valley of mountainous waves and when she rose the lifeboat was capsized with the bottom facing upwards. Some of the men in their oilskins were spotted clambering back on to and sitting astride the upturned boat. But soon after they were seen sliding back into the rough waters as the bitter cold numbed their wet limbs. Others drifted towards the *Palme*, whose own crew launched a small boat in a desperate attempt to save the men, only to see their own boat get smashed to pieces by the waves. Those on board the *Palme* could only watch as the lifeless bodies of the lifeboat men in their oilskins and cork belts washed past their ship.

By this time a second lifeboat the *Hannah Pickard* had also put to sea to help rescue the *Palme*. When it was about 600 yards outside the harbour it too capsized throwing her crew into the water. Both lifeboats were designed to right themselves if capsized but the Civil Service No 7 failed to do so, luckily the *Hannah Pickard* did, and its crew were able to scramble safely back on board. The men continued rowing on toward the *Palme* and their comrades but were unable to get nearer than 400 yards. It was then that they spotted the lifeboat, capsized earlier, which appeared to them to be anchored into the sand, and could see no sign of life. They continued to search for another three quarters of an hour but to no avail, all 15 men were lost.

Further attempts were made to rescue the crew of the *Palme* but it was not until the 26th of December that the captain, his wife and child and 17 crewmen were taken on board an Irish Lights Tender and brought safely into Dún Laoghaire harbour.

At first the bodies of 13 of the lifeboat men were recovered from the sea as the small town was in mourning at the loss of such brave men. The funerals of the 13 were held together on the 28th of December. A sketch accompanied an article in the Evening Herald detailing the mass funeral which showed 13 horse drawn hearses lined up on the Marine Road in Dún Laoghaire. In turn the family and friends stood behind the hearse of each man. The band of the Dublin Metropolitan Police headed the procession followed by the crew of the Palme and various other local maritime groups all slowly walking to the sound of the Dead March. The streets all along the route to the cemetery were lined with throngs of people from near and far who came to pay their respects. As the funeral passed out towards Monkstown, the capsized lifeboat could be still clearly seen stuck upwards in the sand a short distance off the coast.

At the time, Catholics and Protestants were buried separately from one another in Dean's Grange Cemetery. As the procession arrived at the gates the 13 hearses pulled up on the roadway outside. One by one each coffin was removed from their hearse and taken through the gates on the shoulders of local sailors. The coffin of each man was made of polished oak with brass fittings and the simple inscription stating that they each 'Died 24th December, 1895'. The lifeboat crewmen were finally laid to rest on opposite sides of the main walkway of the cemetery, the Catholic men were interred in the North section to the right and those of the Protestant faith, were interred in the South section to the left.

It was not until the 5th of January 1896 that the fourteenth man, William Dunphy was recovered from the sea near the Poolbeg lighthouse in Dublin Bay. Local fishermen discovered his body floating in the water and removed him to Howth harbour.

The body of Henry Williams, the oldest of the crewmen, was also recovered by fishermen off the coast of Howth two weeks later on the 21st of January. The man who had spent the longest time working on the sea would be the one who was kept longest by it in death.

In all there are 14 graves holding the remains of the men of Civil Service No 7. the first, that of father and son Henry and Alexander Williams is in the mind of this writer, the most striking of all in the cemetery and a testimony to the courage of all members of the R.N.L.I. This grave is located directly behind the office. The headstone consists of a large rectangular piece of limestone on top of which is mounted a miniature bronze replica of the lifeboat and bronze anchor. The memorial inscription reads as follows:

'In Memory of Henry and Alexander Williams, Father and Son,
Ex Cox.n and Cox.n of the Kingstown Lifeboat who lost their
lives together at their post in the disaster Xmas Eve 1895.
They nobly did their duty.
Pleasant in their lives and in their death they were not divided.
II. Sam. I. 23.'

This grave is still visited today as is evidenced by a small bouquet of flowers which is regularly placed in the boat.

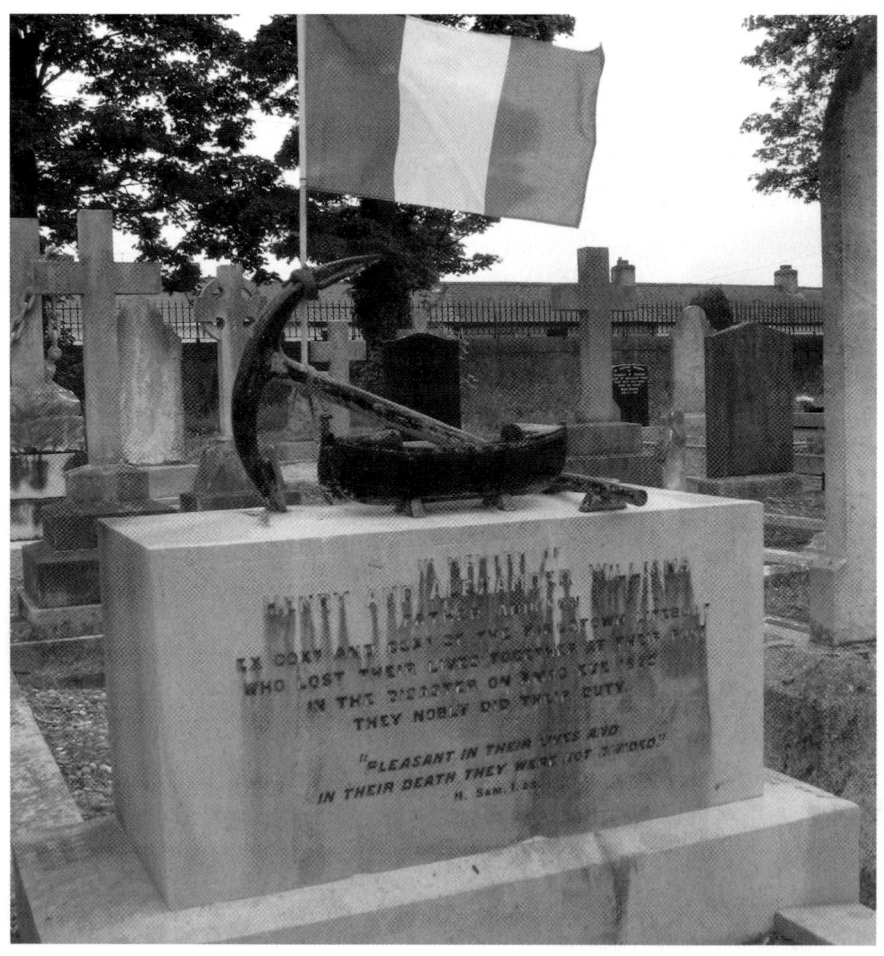

The memorial of Alexander and Henry Williams

Next to the Williams' grave lie those of John Bartley and Henry Underhill and directly facing them on the opposite side of the pathway are the graves of brothers Frank and George Saunders. These four latter headstones are a similar style apart for two unique engravings on those of the Saunders brothers. At the top of each of the brothers' domed shaped marble headstone is a unique engraving, one depicting the lifeboat under sail in heavy seas and the other engraving showing that of the capsized lifeboat.

The headstones on the nine Catholic graves are all identical, consisting of a shouldered tablet headstone, each made of marble and sitting on a limestone base. The nine men are: John Barker, James Ryan, Edward Shannon, Thomas Dunphy, William Dunphy and Edward Murphy buried together side by side while those of Patrick Power, Edward Crowe and Francis McDonald are in different parts of the same section. The following words are inscribed on each of their headstones as well as those of Bartley and Underhill:

'One of the Kingstown Lifeboat crew, who perished in a gallant and heroic attempt to rescue the men of the Russian ship 'Palme' wrecked in Dublin Bay on Xmas Eve 1895.'

Twenty-six dependants were left to fend for themselves as a result of the tragedy. The very day the disaster occurred the people of Dublin began the task of raising funds for the men's families. A meeting organised that Christmas Eve in Dún Laoghaire heard:

'They had sacrificed their lives in a noble endeavour, to save the lives of others, those brave townsmen of ours; they were a credit to their town and their country, and it was for the gentlemen at the meeting to take such steps as would keep want from the doors of their families.'

The following list is taken from the Dean's Grange Cemetery Register of Interments, which records the details of each man.

Name	Age	Address	Occupation	Grave Number
John Barker	38	3 Wellington Place	Sailor	89-I1-North
John Bartley	45	Clarence Street	Sailor	15-N2-South
Edward Crowe	33	11 Tivoli Road	Ships Captain	26-G4-North
William Dunphy	38	Molloy's Court	Fisherman	88-H1-North
Thomas Dunphy	31	Hilton's Court	Fisherman	88-I1-North
Francis McDonald	27	7 Crofton Avenue	Sailor	126-P-North

Edward Murphy	31	Kelly's Court	Sailor	86-I1-North
Patrick Power	23	19 Wellington Street	Sailor	53-I3-North
James Ryan	25	Clarence Street	Sailor	87-H1-North
George B Saunders	31	9 Wellington Street	Sailor	20-H2-South
Francis Saunders	28	11 Clarence Street	Sailor	21-H2-South
Edward Shannon	25	Harbour Yard	Sailor	87-I1-North
Henry Underhill	38	Harbour Yard	Sailor	16-N2-South
Alexander Williams	37	Harbour Yard	Coxwain	17-N2-South
Henry Williams	66	Harbour Yard	Harbour Boatman	17-N2-South

RMS Leinster

'You feeling hearted Christians all in country or in town,
come listen to my doleful song which I have just penned down.
It's all about the war time act that awful tragedy,
when the Dublin Mail Boat Leinster was sunk in the Irish Sea.'

The above words are from a song which is sung by William Byrne a local singer / songwriter. It depicts the scene around the sinking of the Royal Mail Ship *Leinster* during the First World War. William's own Great Grandfather was aboard the ship on that day and clearly William feels a strong and passionate connection between himself and this tragic episode.

On the 10th of October 1918, one month before the end of WWI and at a time when the leaders of the Allied Forces and Germany were in truce negotiations, the single most disastrous incident in the Irish Sea took place.

Earlier that morning the Royal Mail Ship *Leinster* set sail from Dún Laoghaire Harbour bound for Holyhead in North Wales. It is believed that there were a total of 771 people on board the *Leinster*, consisting of 99 members of the City of Dublin Steam Packet Company (C.D.S.P.Co), 180 civilian passengers, and 492 members of the Allied Forces many of whom were on their way to the battle fields.

The sinking of the RMS Leinster

That autumn morning was described as fine but chilly although the sea was reported to be quite rough. By 10am the *Leinster* was roughly 12 miles out from Dún Laoghaire and nearing the Kish lighthouse when, without any warning, a German submarine (UB123) fired a torpedo at the ship. This first torpedo narrowly missed the *Leinster* but the captain of the sub ordered another torpedo be fired and this time he didn't make the same mistake. The second torpedo exploded as it hit the port bow of the *Leinster*, where the ships postal workers were sorting the mail. In total, there were 22 men in the sorting room at this time and all but one of them lost their lives.

As the ship spun out of control, the crew were desperately trying to lower the lifeboats in order to get the passengers to safety. However, within three minutes the German sub fired a third torpedo, this time hitting the engine room with devastating results.

The explosion was so powerful that the ships two engine towers came crashing down on the terrified passengers and crew and she began to sink rapidly. In the panic, attempts to lower the lifeboats were chaotic. A survivor stated that there was 'no chance of getting into any boat in any orderly way'. Most of the boats overturned in the rough sea spilling the passengers into the cold waters where their screams and calls for help could be heard in all directions. Other ships in the vicinity came to the aid of the stricken passengers but it was an hour-and-a-half before boats from Dún Laoghaire Harbour arrived on the scene.

Eyewitness accounts at the time described people floating around or clutching for their lives onto upturned boats or pieces of wreckage. They also described the horrific scenes as people slipped away from whatever little piece of wreckage they were clinging to and disappeared beneath the waves, too cold and numb to hold on any longer. One of the most distressing sights was that of a mother and child as they both drowned after falling from the ship. The four year old girl still had her arms clenched tightly around her mother's neck.

It was not until a number of days after the disaster that the full impact of the sinking and loss of life was fully realised. In all, 501 people were reported lost and the sinking of the *Leinster* was compared to that of the *Titanic* six years previously. Although the number of deaths was not as high as that of the *Titanic*, it was as big a tragedy to the people of Ireland. The largest numbers of deaths were among the military forces. Most of these were Irish or English with a few French, Canadians, Americans, and others. The total numbers of deaths were listed as follows:

Civilian	115	Crew	39
Postal Staff	21	Military	326

Dean's Grange Cemetery holds the final resting places of only a handful of the men and women lost during the sinking of the *Leinster*. At the time of the sinking, Undertakers were on strike and it was feared that this would disrupt the funerals. The strike was settled by the 12th of October and the burials were allowed to go ahead. There

Frank Saunders and his wife, Frances (Fanny) Saunders

are 11 known victims interred in Dean's Grange Cemetery ranging from crew, passengers, and military. Of the 11 people; one stands out in stark contrast to that of the rest, Frances Saunders.

Frances Saunders was the widow of Frank Saunders, one of the crew of the RNLI lifeboat who lost his life in the same waters 23 years earlier during the *Palme* rescue. On foot of a telegram from her daughter's doctor, Frances was travelling over to Holyhead where her daughter Janet was living. Janet had become very ill and Mrs Saunders planned to travel over and help nurse her back to health. Unfortunately tragedy was to hit the family again as Janet died three days after her mother. Both Frances and Janet were buried with Frank Saunders in the family plot in Dean's Grange. Part of the inscription on the headstone reads:

'Also his wife Frances Elizabeth, drowned on RMS Leinster
Oct. 10 1918, aged 51. Peace, Perfect Peace'

Two of the ship's crew were also laid to rest here in Dean's Grange Cemetery. Arthur Jeffries was the ship's wireless operator and Henry Tyrrell the quartermaster, both of them local men from the Dún Laoghaire area.

Arthur Henry Jeffries is believed to have perished in the radio room while sending the SOS distress message as the ship went down. He was aged 27 and was originally from Cambridge, England. At the time of the sinking Arthur lived with his wife Margaret and his step-son Charlie at Mosaster Lodge in Glenageary, Dún Laoghaire. His remains were interred in Dean's Grange on the 15th of October. There is a family memorial on the grave and as Arthur was in the Merchant Navy there is also a CWGC headstone. The family memorial consists of a marble cross sitting on four plinths and is inscribed with the following words from his wife Margaret.

'In memory of my dearly loved husband Arthur Jeffries
who died at sea after sinking of his ship SS Leinster
by German Submarine, 10th Oct 1918. Words fail my loss to tell'

Arthur's grave is located in the far right hand corner of the South-West section, underneath a large Monterey cypress tree.

Henry Tyrrell was one of the ship's quartermasters whose job it was to steer the vessel. He was aged 58 and lived with his wife Bridget at 2 Jane Ville, Tivoli Road in Dún Laoghaire. Henry was originally from Arklow Co Wicklow, another East coast fishing port, and moved to Dún Laoghaire where he married his wife. Bridget also worked as a stewardess with the C.D.S.P.Co but luckily was not on board the *Leinster* at the time. Henry was buried on the 14th of October 1918 and his grave can be found to the right hand side of the main walkway not far inside the main gate. There is a family headstone on the grave made of limestone and which is in the form of a tablet design. A cross is cut out of the top of the stone and the inscription at the base reads:

'In loving memory of Henry Tyrrell Quarter Master of SS Leinster. Who
lost his life in the Leinster disaster in the Irish Channel
on the 10th October 1918 aged 58 years.
Erected by his loving wife Bridget Tyrrell.'

Both Arthur and Henry were buried in family plots. As the men were classed as merchant seamen they each received a headstone by the Commonwealth War Graves Commission, with their name and rank, inscribed below an engraving of the Merchant Navy crest which depicts an anchor surrounded by rope and a crown.

Maud Ward was aged 44 years old and was the personal secretary to the Count of Carysfort, Colonel Douglas Proby. It is believed she was travelling from the Carysfort estate outside Arklow Co Wicklow to her family home in Birmingham, England when the ship was torpedoed. Her grave and funeral arrangements were paid for by the Colonel who is said to have taken the news of her death like that of one of his own family. Maud's own family erected a granite cross headstone on the grave which is near to the centre of the South-West section, the inscription reads

'Maud Elizabeth Ward born June 12 1874,
drowned on SS Leinster October 10 1918.
He sent from above, he took me, he drew me out of many waters.'

Christina Goodman was the first of the victims to be buried in the cemetery. Christina was a 64 year old single lady who was travelling back to her home in Parliament Street in Liverpool. Her remains were buried in a plot owned by a local family named Comas. This grave can be found a few spaces beyond the office on the main walkway. Her inscription which is inscribed on the side of the Comas monument reads:

'In loving memory of Christina Goodman,
Drowned in the sinking of RMS Leinster, Oct 10. 1918.
There was no more sea'

Patrick O'Toole was employed as a fireman with the City of Dublin Steam Packet Company and tended to the boilers on board the *Leinster*.

He lived with his parents James and Catherine at 1 Summerhill Avenue in Sandycove. His funeral was held on the 13th of October in Dean's Grange Cemetery where his coffin was carried behind the hearse on the shoulders of his comrades from the C.D.S.P. Co His grave is just off the pathway between the West and upper North and is marked by a large limestone memorial engraved with the following inscription:

'Patrick, who lost his life in the Leinster disaster,
in the Irish Channel on 10th October 1918, aged 23 years'

Dorothy May Jones lived at Charleville in Dalkey and was on a personal journey to England when the ship was struck. She was a member of the St Johns Ambulance Association and served as a Voluntary Aid Detachment nurse during the war. She was nursing at a military hospital in France and returned home during the summer. Dorothy's remains were not discovered until mid-November and they were later interred on the 17th in her Grandfathers grave in the South section, on the opposite side of the pathway to the Protestant chapel. Her inscription on the large marble headstone reads as follows:

'In proud and loving memory of his Granddaughter, Dorothy May Jones, V.A.D. Lost in the sinking of the Leinster 10th October 1918, aged 27 years. Thy kingdom come, and, as in heaven, on earth thy will be done.'

Emily Barlow was aged 42 when she died. She was originally from Riverstown Co Sligo and was travelling home to Mostyn in Cheshire, England on the day of the sinking. Her remains are buried in the South-West section and her headstone has the following inscription:

'In loving memory of, Emily E. Barlow,
lost on the Leinster, Oct. 10. 1918.
In thy presence is fullness of joy'

The headstone is a small marble tablet measuring no more than 18' inches high and there are no surrounds on the grave. It is positioned under the same large cypress tree as Arthur Jeffries in the far corner of the section.

Robert Ernest Lee served as a captain with the Royal Army Medical Corps of the British Army and was in the process of travelling to England at the time of the sinking. Robert was home on leave and visiting his parents Annie and Edward of Bellevue, Blackrock. He was buried in the family's double plot in the South section and his grave is marked with a limestone cross and plinth. There is a second headstone on the double plot which is located behind the offices, where half way along the path it turns off to the right. The inscriptions are an eye opener to the realities and harshness of life even within a wealthy family like his. The inscriptions also state that his brother Joseph died at Gallipoli in 1915, and whose remains were never brought home. His mother and Father are also buried here as well as five of his siblings who all died under fivemonths of age. The following words are inscribed on his headstone:

Capt. Robert Ernest Lee

'In loving memory of Robert Ernest Lee, Captain R.A.M.C.
lost in the sinking of RMS Leinster Oct. 10. 1918, aged 35 years.
Faithful unto death'

Robert's name is also listed on the Great War Memorial in Baggot Street Hospital where it says he was a 'student and life governor'.

Elizabeth Ellam, who was from Essex in England, was returning home from a holiday with her daughter and son-in-law in Skibbereen, Co Cork. Her son-in-law, who was a dentist, was only able to identify her by her teeth. The inscription on the marble headstone reads:

'In loving memory of mother
Elizabeth Ellam,
killed in the Leinster
Oct. 10. 1918.
A good and beautiful woman
has passed on'

Elizabeth Ellam

Elizabeth's grave is located close to that of Maud Ward in the centre of the South-West section.

A local man named William John Smith was working in the engine room of the *Leinster* when she was sunk. John, who was aged 49, lived with his wife Mary at 17 Desmond Avenue in Dún Laoghaire. His occupation is listed in the cemetery records as that of a fireman, but at the time he was working as a greaser while on the *Leinster*. His remains were interred in Dean's Grange Cemetery on the 14th of October 1918.

John's name appears on the Tower Hill Memorial in London as a Mercantile Marine who was lost at sea, the memorial states…

'who has no grave but the sea'.

John Smith, indeed, has a grave and is buried at the far edge of the West section alongside that of St Brigid but sadly it has no headstone.

I feel I should mention at this time William Maher and John Donohoe, two heroes of the *Leinster* disaster. If it wasn't for the courage of these men and others, there would surely have been further loss of life in the event. John and William saved a number of people's lives that day. Both men survived the sinking and lived for many years, the two men are now buried in Dean's Grange Cemetery. (See chapter on Notable People for William Maher)

1916 Rising

'We declare the right of the people of Ireland to the ownership of Ireland, and to the unfettered control of Irish destinies, to be sovereign and indefeasible. The long usurpation of that right by a foreign people and government has not extinguished the right, nor can it ever be extinguished except by the destruction of the Irish people.'

An excerpt from the Proclamation of Independence 1916

An event took place in Dublin on Easter Monday, the 24th of April 1916, that would change the course of Britain's involvement in Ireland for ever and become a pivotal stepping stone in the direction of Irish independence.

A nationalist group known as the Irish Volunteers undertook military action in order to overthrow British rule in Ireland in the event that became known as the 1916 Easter Rising. On that Monday, the Irish Volunteers occupied strategic positions in and around the capital and using the General Post Office on O'Connell Street as their Head Quarters, declared an Irish Republic. Of the estimated 10,000 Irish Volunteers originally ordered to mobilise that day, somewhere between 1,500 and 2,000 took part with Cumann na mBan and na Fianna Eireann members also in the ranks.

For five long days and nights Dublin city became a battleground between the small group of republican nationalists and the far superior

British forces, who couldn't have believed for one minute that they would be fighting a war in their own back garden. Over 20,000 British troops poured into the capital in the following days, but the Volunteers defended their positions well and inflicted considerable casualties on their foe.

At 3.45pm on Saturday the 29th of April, Pádraic Pearse, commander of the Volunteers signed an unconditional surrender. Pearse took this decision in the hope of preventing the further slaughter of the citizens of Dublin at the hands of the British forces as well as to save the lives of his comrades. In the immediate weeks after the rising, Pearse and another 15 leading republicans would pay the ultimate price.

From the day the Volunteers surrendered, Dean's Grange Cemetery, which is situated only a few miles south of the Dublin city centre, began to take in some of the victims of the rising. It was recorded in the minutes of a meeting held by the Dean's Grange Joint Burial Board on the 12th of May 1916 that:

> *'...report from the Registrar stating that a number of bodies were sent by the military authorities & buried in this cemetery without coffins.'*

More than 450 people had died during the fighting, of whom about 50 were interred in Dean's Grange Cemetery. It was impossible to obtain coffins for the majority of these victims, and of the bodies brought to this cemetery, most were buried without coffins and some were lucky if they had even a simple sheet wrapped around them.

Six of the first victims who were brought in by a military truck were buried together in what was later to become known as the 1916 Plot. This plot is situated in the West section and is located directly in from the Republican Plot. It is about three quarters of the way along the path and can be found on the left hand side, surrounded by a chain link. The 1916 Plot is probably one of the most significant of its kind in Ireland because of those buried there. It consists of a republican

National Graves Association headstone that resembles a scroll and also a Commonwealth War Graves Commission headstone, each at opposite ends of the plot. Both memorials are carved from limestone and the plot is surrounded by a chain link, in which the six men were all buried on the 1st of May 1916. Of the six who were intered here, three were civilians, two were republican Volunteers, and one was a British soldier. I am not aware of any other location in the country where members of these two opposing sides are buried together.

Joseph Costello and Andrew Byrne were the two Volunteers. Joseph Costello was only 22 years of age and held the rank of 2nd Lieutenant of the Irish Volunteers. He was a native of Athlone, Co Westmeath, but was living and working in the capital for the previous two years. On the third day of the Rising, Joseph was carrying dispatches to Boland's Mills, which was under Irish Volunteer control. While making his way

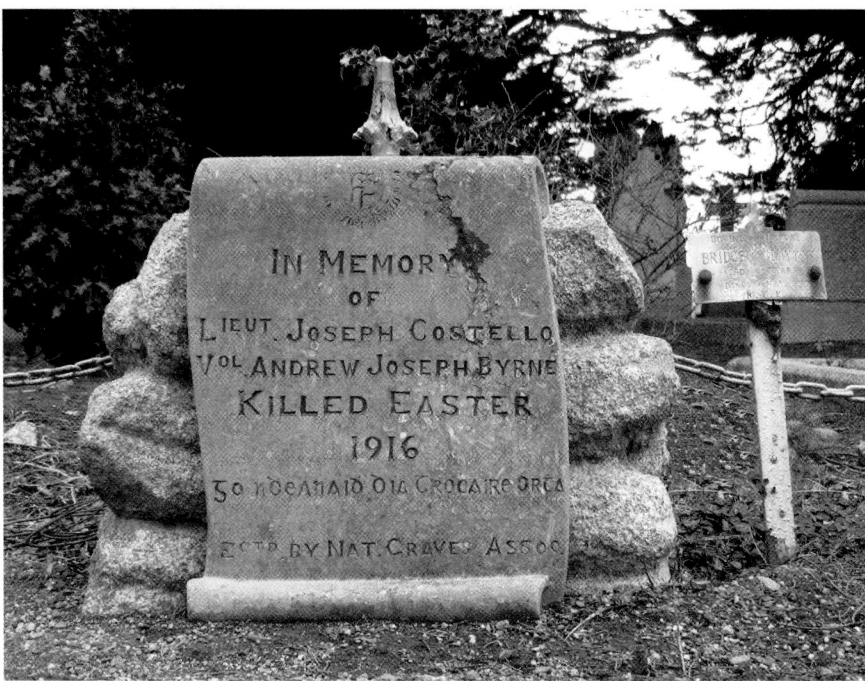

Headstone marking the graves of Joseph Costello and Andrew Byrne.

along Grand Canal Street towards the Mills, he was shot by one of the British soldiers who had taken up positions around the Mills. The authorities allowed the wounded man to be moved the short distance to Sir Patrick Dun's Hospital, where he died later that day, the 26th of April. His comrade Andrew Byrne, of the 3rd Battalion Irish Volunteers was also shot by sniper fire in the Boland's Mills area, and died on Thursday the 27th of April. Both names are inscribed on the headstone which is in the centre of the plot. Part of the inscription is in Gaelic, and this asks God to have mercy on their souls.

The British soldier who was also interred in this plot was a 33 year old Private in the 1st Battalion Scots Guards named Peter Ennis. A native of Dublin, Peter was home on leave when the fighting broke out on Easter Monday. It was reported that on that Easter Tuesday, the 25th of April, Peter was out walking in the Mount Street area near Boland's Mills and must have been completely unaware of the presence of the Volunteers. At around 3pm he was walking along Clanwilliam Place and as he came up outside Sir Patrick Dun's Hospital a shot rang out. Peter was still wearing his British Army uniform when the Volunteers spotted him passing the gates of the hospital. Peter's military headstone faces that of the two Volunteers in the 1916 Plot. The Scots Guards crest on Peter's memorial consists of a four pointed badge and four tartan sections with a thistle at the centre. Circled around the thistle is the motto '*Nemo me impune lacessit*' which translates as 'No one assails me with impunity'.

The three other men buried in the 1916 Plot were all civilians, John Kenyon, Joseph Clarke, and William Carrick. I could find no information as to where these men lost their lives, only that they each died of gun shot wounds.

When the fighting first broke out on the Monday and the Irish Volunteers took over the General Post Office, it didn't take long for the rising to claim its first casualties. That afternoon, as the Volunteers had just finished barricading themselves into the GPO, a group of Volunteers from Rathfarnham in South Dublin, who arrived late, decided to make a dash across O'Connell Street from North Earl Street in order to gain access to the Headquarters. At the same time, a group of British Lancers on horseback were riding down from the top of O'Connell Street to survey the situation, when they spotted the Volunteers hurrying across the road. The Lancers, realising the difficulty the men were experiencing in getting into the GPO, charged at them and caused the Volunteers to panic. The Volunteers responded by firing on the approaching Lancers, killing three of them immediately and fatally wounding another.

In this engagement, one of the Volunteers from Rathfarnham, John Keely, was wounded as he tried to gain entry to the Post Office through one of the lower windows. John was a 30 year old married man from Rockbrook, Ballyboden and was a staunch lover of the Gaelic language. He taught Irish in the Gaelic League in Dún Laoghaire and also taught with Francis Macken in St Enda's School, run by Pádraic Pearse. The wounded man was taken to Jervis Street Hospital but died there early the following morning. He was one of the first of over 60 Volunteers to die as a result of the Rising. His body was removed to Dean's Grange Cemetery for burial on the 1st of May and interred in the upper North section just in from the Consecration Cross.

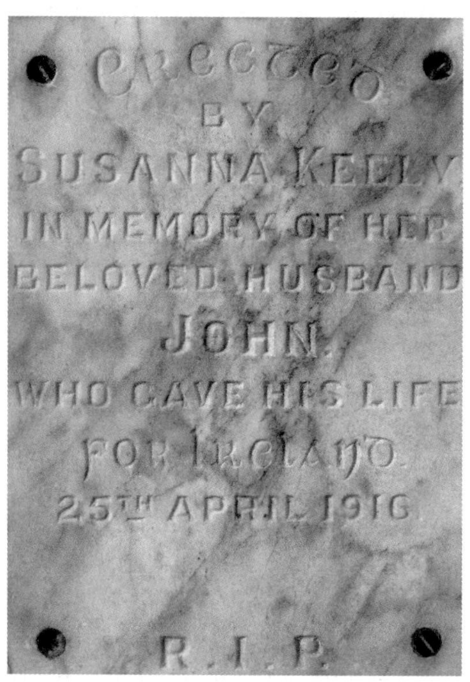

John Keely inscription

Today John's grave is marked by a statue of Jesus standing on a pillar which has the following inscription etched into a marble plaque at the base (see photo on previous page):

'Erected by Susanna Keely in memory of her beloved husband John who gave his life for Ireland 25th April 1916.'

At about the same time in the south of the city another Dubliner was shot and killed. The Irish Volunteers shot and killed a soldier, John Mulhern, a rifleman with the 3rd Battalion Royal Irish Rifles. He was shot not far from where he and his wife Annie lived with their children at 6 St Stephen's Place, just off Lower Mount Street. His details were not entered into the cemetery records until October 1920, such was the confusion surrounding the Rising. Although his age is inscribed as 40 on the CWGC headstone, he was in fact aged 32. His burial plot is located at the far end of the West section and is only a few graves in from the pathway near the large cypress conifer at its junction with the South-West.

To the south of Dublin city that afternoon the Home Defence Force, were involved in mock training exercises in the Dublin Mountains, when word reached them that the 'Sinn Feiners' (Volunteers) had declared an Irish Republic and taken control of the city. Named 'Georgius Rex', they were more commonly referred to by Dublin citizens as 'Gorgeous Wrecks', because their membership mainly consisted of elderly men and war veterans of Dublin's upper classes. While training that day, the GRs were wearing their military uniforms and carrying rifles. Although they had no ammunition for the guns they still decided to march towards Dublin.

When the GRs reached Ballsbridge, they took the decision to split into two groups. The larger of these headed towards Sandymount while the smaller, led by second-in-command Francis Browning headed for

Beggars Bush Barracks via Northumberland Road and Haddington Road. As the men travelled on foot along Northumberland Road toward the junction of Haddington Road, they were unaware that Volunteers, under the command of Michael Malone, had anticipated that this would be a route taken by British forces from the port of Dún Laoghaire. When the GRs were within range they came under fire from the Volunteers positioned in house number 25 Northumberland Road. Francis Browning and four of his men were shot and lay dead or wounded in the street. When the Volunteers in number 25 realised that they were indeed the Home Guard and that they were not carrying ammunition in which to return fire, they ceased their attack and permitted the wounded to be taken to houses on the opposite side of the road.

Francis Browning

Francis Browning was aged 47 and died two days later on the 26th of April from a single wound he received to the head. His remains were later buried in the Browning family plot in Dean's Grange Cemetery. Here, on the grave situated not far from the Protestant Chapel, members of the Irish Rugby Football Union Volunteers Corps, erected an impressive monument in his memory. The following inscription is etched on the large rectangular limestone block which marks the grave and which has a plinth and cross positioned above it:

'This stone has been erected by the members of the Irish Rugby Football Union Volunteer Corps, in affectionate remembrance of Francis Henry Browning B.A. Barrister-at-Law, its founder and commanding officer, and 2nd in Command of the 1st (Dublin) Battalion of the Irish Association of Volunteer Training Corps. He died from wounds received at Northumberland Road Dublin during the Sinn Féin rising of Easter Week 1916, while returning with his

men to Beggars Bush Barracks. He will live in the memory of all as an honourable comrade, and true and distinguished sportsman, who by his untiring efforts and splendid patriotism obtained from his Corps over 300 recruits for His Majesty's Forces during the Great European War. Born 22nd June 1868. Died 26th April 1916.'

It was reported that on the following morning Tuesday the 25th of April, a car travelling in the direction of the city was called upon to stop by Volunteers as it approached Mount Street Bridge. At the time the car was driven by an officer of the Royal Army Medical Corps who refused to obey the request to stop and who tried to drive on through. The men occupying Clanwilliam House, directly opposite the bridge, immediately fired on the car as it tried to cross the bridge, bringing it to a sudden stop above the canal. Unknown to the Volunteers, the officer had offered a lift that morning to an official of the Bank of Ireland, College Green. Richard Waters was travelling into work from his house in Blackrock when the volley of shots struck the car, causing him serious injury. The officer escaped unhurt and the wounded bank official was removed by ambulance to Sir Patrick Dun's Hospital where he died a short time later.

Richard Waters had never married and it was left to his sister to organise the purchase of his grave and headstone. There is a very interesting piece from the inscription in which she describes how her brother died.

'In loving memory of Richard Waters of Recess Blackrock,
shot by the rebels on his way to his office 25th April 1916.
Erected by his sister to the dearest and best of brothers.
Father in Thy tender keeping, Leave I now my loved one sleeping.'

Because of the killing of Francis Browning, Richard Waters, and others throughout the city, Pádraic Pearse issued a command that the Volunteers were not to fire on any person, including British soldiers who carried no ammunition as they were deemed unarmed.

Later that same evening one of the most controversial incidents of that Easter week had begun to unfold. A captain with the British army's Royal Irish Rifles by the name of John C. Bowen-Colthurst oversaw the arrest of three men, as alleged sympathisers of the Volunteers.

The three men were, Francis Sheehy-Skeffington, a famous Dublin pacifist and Socialist, Thomas Dickson the editor of *The Eye-opener* newspaper and Patrick McIntyre, also the editor of a newspaper called *The Searchlight*. The three men were taken to Portobello Barracks and placed in detention cells over night. At around 10am the following morning, Captain Bowen-Colthurst returned to the men's cells and ordered the three to walk into the detention yard, which was directly adjacent to their cell. He also ordered seven soldiers from the detention block to take their rifles and follow him into the yard. The three prisoners were then told to walk to the far end of the small yard, which was only 40 by 15 feet, and as they did ao, Bowen-Colthurst turned to the seven soldiers and ordered them to shoot the three men just as they reached the yard wall.

Bowen-Colthurst's explanation for ordering the killings was that he feared the barracks would come under attack by the Irish Volunteers in trying to free the three men. Later on during the day, the bodies of the three men were buried in a pit in the barracks yard. It was not until mid-May 1916 that their bodies were exhumed for proper burial. The remains of Patrick McIntyre were brought to Dean's Grange Cemetery on the 19th of May and interred in a grave opposite the 1916 Plot in the West section. There is no headstone on Patrick's grave which sits under a tall conifer tree just to the left of the pathway.

The Simon commission of inquiry, which was set up to investigate the shooting of these men found that all three had no part whatsoever to play in the rising. This is not surprising as *The Searchlight*, of which Patrick McIntyre was editor, was a staunchly loyalist newspaper and supported the recruiting campaign for the First World War, and so opposed the Irish Volunteers. In June 1919, John C. Bowen-Colthurst was found guilty of the murders of the three men and of another three who were killed at separate times during the rising. He was deemed insane and was removed to Broadmoor Asylum in England. From there he was quickly transferred to another hospital in Canada where he was released in April 1921 after serving only twenty months detention. The Royal Irish Rifles captain was found to be 'cured', and was officially discharged from the British Army and received a full pension by the age of 40.

On the same day as Patrick McIntyre and the other two men were shot, the British army were in the process of moving scores of troops out of the port of Dún Laoghaire. The troops landed there the night before and now marched towards the city and straight into battle with the Volunteers. Before they could enter the city, the soldiers had to overcome the republican held strongholds of Northumberland Road and Mount Street Bridge and it was here that the British Army would suffer their heaviest casualties.

As the first party of soldiers from the Sherwood Foresters were led up Northumberland Road towards its junction with Haddington Road, Volunteers positioned in number 25 Northumberland Road opened fire, claiming the first of many British casualties. Captain Frederick Christian Dietrichsen of the 2nd/7th Battalion was one of two soldiers who died in that first attack. Only a short time before, as the soldiers marched towards the city from Dún Laoghaire, Capt Dietrichsen noticed his wife and two children

Captain Frederick Dietrichsen

standing on the side of the road waving to the soldiers as they passed by. Unknown to Frederick, his wife Beatrice had brought the children over to stay with relatives in Dublin in order to escape the zeppelin raids. Dietrichsen dropped out of rank and threw his arms around his family, not knowing that this would be the last time they would meet.

Fredrick Dietrichsen was 33 years of age and had worked as a Barrister in England before joining the army during the First World War. He died in the house at number 26 Northumberland Road. On the 29th of April the Army removed his remains from Baggot Street Hospital and had them interred in Dean's Grange Cemetery. His grave is located just off the pathway which leads behind the cemetery offices. The memorial basically consists of granite surrounds with no headstone. Particular attention should be paid to the granite surrounds of the grave for it is on these that his epithet is inscribed. Although the words have become worn over the years I believe they read as follows:

'Frederick Christian Dietrichsen,
Cap 2/7 Sherwood Foresters (robin hoods),
Killed in action in Dublin April 26th 1916,
A soldier does not choose the place or ways to serve Christ'

During continuous attempts to oust the Volunteers from this area, more and more Sherwood Foresters were falling to the Volunteer's rifles. Later on in the day as the Sherwood Foresters cleared a way up Northumberland Road and were trying to get across Mount Street Bridge, they again came under fire from Volunteers this time in Clanwilliam House on the opposite side of the canal, from where Richard Waters was shot.

In an attempt to cross the bridge and take the house by storm, a number of the Sherwood Foresters were gunned down with the remainder forced to retreat. Montague Bernard Browne a Second Lieutenant of the 2nd/8th Battalion was fatally wounded on the North-West corner of the bridge as he and another Lieutenant of the 2nd/8th led the attack.

Browne was a single man who lived with his mother at their family home named Rutland House in North Collingham, Nottingham. He died two days later in hospital, and was buried in the South-West section of Dean's Grange Cemetery, along with a private J.S. Blissett of the 2nd/7th Battalion, who died during the same attack. Blissett was buried along with M.B. Browne on the 1st of May in the Cemetery's South-West section. The grave is marked by a large limestone Celtic cross which was erected by Browne's family. Browne's inscription is on the face of the monument with Blissett's inscription engraved to the side. The grave containing the two soldiers is positioned under the shadow of a large Monterey cypress conifer which can be found to the far right hand corner of the section. The base of the Celtic cross bears the following inscription:

M. B. Browne

'In loving memory of
Montague Bernard Browne of Collingham Notts,
2nd Lieut. 2/8 Sherwood Foresters,
who died in hospital April 28th 1916
from wounds received in action in Dublin
on April 26th during the Irish rebellion, Age 39.
Be thou faithful unto death,
and I will give thee a crown of life'
'Also in memory of
Private J.S. Blissett of Nottingham,
2/7 Sherwood Foresters
who fell at the same time age 23.
'Till He Come'

J. S. Blissett

Over 200 soldiers mainly of the Sherwood Foresters either died or were wounded between 25 Northumberland Road and Clanwilliam House. Their commanders could easily have ordered the men to take another route towards the city but the tactic of the time was to force soldiers onward, as they had done in France and Belgium. As it later turned out, many of these young men had only just undergone training in the previous six weeks and some weren't even sure of how to load their rifles. The soldiers own lack of experience and ill judged tactics ordered by their senior commanding officer General Lowe resulted in the slaughter by a small detachment of Volunteers.

Dublin was not the only part of Ireland to see fighting that Easter week. In Co Meath, Irish Volunteers under the command of Thomas Ashe had planned an attack on the police barracks in the small village of Ashbourne. Volunteers took up positions around the barracks but not long after their attack began, they were forced to defend themselves against a separate patrol of Royal Irish Constabulary officers who had come on the scene.

As the battle ensued, two commercial travellers from Dún Laoghaire, James Joseph Carroll, and Jeremiah (Gerald St John) Hogan attempted to drive their car through the town and were both shot and killed in the cross fire. The two men were returning home to Dublin on the 28th of April when they got caught up in the fighting at the Ashbourne crossroads. The men's bodies were later conveyed to Dún Laoghaire and buried on the 2nd of May in adjoining graves in the West section, between the present day Republican Plot and the Consecration Cross.

That same day as soldiers of the South Staffordshire Regiment were in the process of placing a cordon around the Four Courts, they came under heavy fire from Volunteers positioned in houses in the nearby North King Street area, to the rear of the Courts. In this engagement a private in the South Staffs, Charles Saunders was killed. Over the next 24 hours many more soldiers were to meet the same fate around the Courts. Saunders who was stationed with the 2nd/6th Battalion died on the 28th of April. His remains were buried in Dean's Grange on the 2nd of May along with Alfred Ellis of the Royal Dublin Fusiliers. The plot with both military headstones side by side lies in the far right hand corner of the section.

The following morning just before Padraic Pearse was to issue an unconditional surrender, the South Staffs had made no progress in getting through North King Street, so the commanding officer decided on a different tactic. Instead of taking the risk of sending soldiers up the street they would literality go through the houses. They occupied one of the first block of houses and from there they broke trough the walls between each building thus making a safe passage towards the Volunteers, who by this time were long gone. Infuriated that the Volunteers dispersed before they got the chance to tackle them, the British soldiers turned their aggression toward the North King Street residents and a total of 15 men and boys were either shot or bayoneted to death in what was to become known as the North King Street massacres.

Among the 15 victims were a father and son who lived in number 168, Thomas Hickey a 38 year old butcher and his young son Christopher Hickey aged 16. Although the military authorities were aware that the massacre had taken place, they only investigated the murders after eyewitness accounts began to spread throughout the city in the days after the Rising. The true horrors were literality unearthed as bodies were found buried in shallow graves. During an inquest into the killings, Kate Kelly who was in the house with Thomas and Christopher Hickey and another friend named Peter Connolly stated that soldiers entered number 168 after breaking through the wall from the adjoining house. All four were then ordered to go next door where the three men were separated into another room. Kate said that she could hear young Christopher pleading with the soldiers not to shoot his father just before a number of shots were fired. The soldiers shot the three innocent men dead in the back room knowing that they played no part in the Rising. Thomas and Christopher were buried in Dean's

Grange Cemetery on the 3rd of May 1916. The only marker for their grave was a mature Monterey cypress conifer which was at the edge of the West section close to that of St Brigid's. The tree was cut down along with many others in late 2008.

As it was at the start of the rising, with the killing of John Keely and John Mulhern so it would end the same way. On the 1st of May two young soldiers, that were buried in this cemetery died in hospital, from gunshot wounds they received during the fighting. The first of these was a 24 year old Irish Volunteer named Andrew Cunningham. Andrew was a silk weaver by trade, and joined the Volunteers when they were first established in 1913. A native of Dublin, Andrew was shot close to his home on the Ringsend Road in the south of the city. His grave is close to that of Thomas and Christopher Hickey. Like the father and son there is no headstone on this Volunteer's grave. The only marker is that of a wooden cross erected by local Republicans who wished to commemorate his sacrifice. The second victim was a soldier named Alfred Ellis, a 19 year old private in the 5th Battalion Royal Dublin Fusiliers. Alfred was from Leeds in England where he lived with his parents Sarah and Alfred senior. He died in hospital on the 1st of May 1916 from gunshot wounds received during the fighting. His remains were buried along with those of Private Charles Saunders. The grave is situated behind that of the two Sherwood Foresters Browne and Blissett in the far right hand corner of the South-West Section.

There were more victims of the fighting that also came to be interred in the cemetery after the rising. I could find very little about the circumstances that led to their deaths only that each had died of gunshot wounds.

John Doyle was aged 20 and lived at 104 Ringsend Road, Dublin. It was recorded in the Interment Records that he worked as a Ppainter and that he died on the 3rd of May 1916. His remains were taken to the cemetery by the military authorities and buried in 30 E1 West. The grave is to the centre LHS of the section.

William Gregg was 64 years old and worked as a bottle maker in Dublin city. He lived at 2 Simpson's Lane, Dublin and was reported killed on the 29th of April while walking along Irishtown Road. His remains were buried in grave 34 S3 West, located near the far right hand corner of the section on the 3rd of May 1916.

Mary Kelly was aged 12 when she died during Easter week 1916. The young girl who lived on Townsend Street in Dublin died from gunshot wounds on the 30th of April. Her remains were interred in grave 9 A2 West which is situated near to the intersection with the North.

Margaret McGuinness was 50 years old and lived at 27 Pembroke Cottages, Dublin. She died in hospital from her wounds on the 3rd of May and was buried in 92 T3 North. She was buried with her husband Joseph who had died two years previously. Their grave is located at the top of the upper North close to the Plot of the Angels.

Bridget Stewart was aged 11 and lived with her family at 3 Pembroke Place, Dublin. She died on the 28th of April and was interred in grave 25 N3 West. She was the youngest of five children born to Charles and Maria Stewart. Her grave is not far from the 1916 Plot, close to St Brigid's section.

George Synnot was 58 years of age and is worked as an official in Dublin. He lived at 98 Haddington Road Dublin and left behind his wife Agnes and two grownup children. George died on the 30th of April and was buried in 96 R South-West. The grave, which is in the centre of the section, also holds the remains of his wife who died in 1938. Below his name are inscribed the words *'Until the day break and the shadows flee away'*

John Flynn was 66 years of age and from Dodder View in Dublin. His remains were interred on the 29th of April in grave 105 K North, which is situated in the centre of the lower North.

There is a report in the cemetery minute book dated July 1916 relating to this period of our history. The Burial Board refused to grant permission for the exhumation and re-interment of the remains of one of the victims, Christopher O'Flaherty. The Board could not consent to this as his remains were interred with other bodies (all victims of the recent fighting) and without coffins, they considered the grave's open exposure to be too dangerous for the public's health. Christopher O'Flaherty was buried along with John Flynn in 105 K North.

Close by is another grave which was used to bury more victims of the rising, two men and a woman. Kate Walsh and Richard Woodcock's bodies were brought from Sir Patrick Dun's Hospital and Joseph Shargine from St Vincent's Hospital. The three victims were recorded as having been buried on the 29th of April but their names were not entered into the cemetery Interment records until July 1918. This was over two months after the rising and only came to light because of the emergence of hospital records. The three were buried in grave 124 K. In all, 49 people who died from gunshot wounds were listed as having been interred in Dean's Grange Cemetery after the rising. To date the exact grave locations of 32 of the victims are known, but the remainder were buried in unmarked graves of which no known record was ever kept. The bodies of twelve of the unknown people were brought to the cemetery from four hospitals on the south side of they city, some of these are known but no grave for these can be identified.

In the graves that cannot be found it is known that the following people now rest.

William Lang was a private with the 2nd/7th Battalion Sherwood Foresters and died on the 26th of April. Because the soldier's grave was never located, the Commonwealth War Graves Commission erected a special memorial between the West and South-West sections of the cemetery. The commission believe that his body was interred along with others in an unmarked grave close to his fellow soldiers.

On the military memorial are inscribed the words *'W. Lang / Believed to be buried in this cemetery'* His regiments crests, which is also on the memorial consists of an eight pointed star badge beneath a crown; this has a stag and the regiment's name at the centre.

Three others, David Swords, Joseph McGuire & John Loughlin where all brought from Sir Patrick Dun's Hospital to the cemetery and buried in unmarked graves.

A final victim's last address was listed as Island Bridge Barracks, 54 year old John McCarthy. Again I could find no information about John, whether he was a local man working as a stable hand or seeking refuge during the fighting remains unclear, but like a lot of the information at the time it is not exact and at times the wrong names are recorded. It would generally be accepted that after the rising the authorities would have been more concerned with burying the victims and preventing the spread of diseases than keeping exact records.

Incidentally, on the 4th of May, a woman by the name of Mary Dwyer was entered into the cemetery records as having been buried that day. Mary was aged 73 and died on the 25th of April and her address was given as Brunswick Street in the centre of Dublin. There is no record of her death occurring as a result of the fighting but regardless of whether this was the case or not; it shows the length of time it took to have people buried.

In the weeks immediately following the Rising, the British authorities executed 16 of the Volunteer leaders which caused the people's anger to turn against them. The added news of atrocities which were carried out by a handful of British soldiers during the week of the Rising didn't help the growing resentment either. With the fear of conscription also hanging above the heads of the Irish people the next five years were going to prove to be a difficult time for England and it's involvement in Irish affairs.

British War Graves

'They shall not grow old, as we that are left grow old:
Age shall not weary them, nor the years condemn.
At the going down of the sun and in the morning,
we will remember them,
we will remember them.'

The above verse is taken from the poem 'For the Fallen' by Laurence Binyon and is synonymous with those who remember their fallen comrades in the British armed forces.

The fact that there are 102 British war graves within the walls of Dean's Grange Cemetery will come as a surprise to most people. When we think of those that have died during the 1st and 2nd World Wars, people generally tend to picture rows of headstones in the military cemeteries of France or Belgium and not to pass a thought that these wars in some way could have reached Ireland. But reach they did in more ways than one.

Some of those that are buried here served in England and received injuries there during both wars. There are also those who were wounded during fighting in France. They mainly died while convalescing in Irish hospitals or later after returning home when they were discharged from the armed forces. There are also those that died as a result of military action in Ireland during the 1916 Rising and the War of Independence. But it would have to be said that most of those 101 men and the one woman died as a result of accidents or illnesses received while on active service. For instance during the latter half of 1918 through 1919 there was a world wide influenza epidemic in which more people died than were killed in the war itself. A search of the internment records of October 1918 shows a marked increase of burials to that of the previous October. 48 people were interred during October 1917 compared to 206 during the same month of the following year which clearly shows the devastating effects the epidemic had on the people.

In the following pages I have listed each person in chronological order of their surname. I have tried to list details regarding their age, marital status, place of residence, military regiments and whereabouts within the cemetery they are buried and a description of their memorials. With regard to the directions given, the starting point is from the nearest gate.

My research shows some differences between the cemetery records and those of the Commonwealth War Graves Commission which are mainly to do with ages and names. In such cases I have chosen to list the details that are inscribed on the memorials before that on record, unless there is an obvious or significant difference.

Although I have only listed those that died on active service, there are many more buried here who took part in these wars and only in later life became interred in Dean's Grange. My own Great-Grandfather James Moran served with the Irish Guards in France during the First World War. He was wounded by a piece of shrapnel, from a mortar shell and spent the remainder of his life with the scars. He died after a long and good life in 1938. Frank Byrne from Stillorgan is another soldier who died during the 2nd World War. Although he is not buried in the cemetery his family has remembered him by including his name on their own headstone. He died in May 1943 at the Japanese controlled 'Formosa Internment Camp' in Taiwan. Many more headstones throughout the cemetery bear the names of soldiers who perished in the two wars and whose bodies could never be returned home.

Below are their comrades…

The Hon. Hector John Atkinson served as a captain in the Royal Irish Fusiliers. He died in Dublin on the 26th of May 1917 at the age of 37. Hector was a past student of Trinity College Dublin and had served with the Fusiliers since joining the force in 1900. He fought in the Boer War and earned a Queen's Medal with three claps and a King's with two claps for his part. During the early period of the First World War, Hector had served in France and in the two years before his death was mainly stationed between Dublin and Belfast. It was while he was home on leave in May 1917 that he died. He was the third son of Lady Jane and Lord John Atkinson, andwas married to Sybil Atkinson of 5 William's Place, Rathmines.

He was buried in grave 75 P South-West on the 29th of May. The headstone is marble and is ornately decorated in a gothic style which sits on a double family plot, also containing his mother and father.

George Henderson Baird was a captain in the Royal Army Medical Corps. He died on the 9th of November 1919 at the age of 56 and was buried in 36 K2 South on the 13th of November.

George used his skill as a doctor with the British Army's medical corps during the war. He was married to Alice Baird of Hawkwood, Woolwich Road, Charlton, Kent and formally lived at his family's residence at Adelaide, Sandymount Castle, Dublin. It was here at the family home that George died.

The marble headstone that marks the grave has a three tier plinth on which sits a cross inscribed with the words *'God Bless you through Eternity'*.

Daniel Barry (service number T/278022) served as a private with the 365th Motor Transport Company, Royal Army Service Corps. He died at the age of 27 on the 3rd of November 1917 and was buried on the 7th of November in grave 11 C3 West. The last address given for

Barry, in the cemetery records is King Georges Hospital. His grave has a standard military Commonwealth War Graves headstone, on which his service number is inscribed, as do most of the military headstones. Someone still visits here as there is a small potted plant buried in the soil and the grave has a wooden surround.

Herbert Bell (service numberMB/776) was a chief motor mechanic on board H.M. Motor Lighter 154. He was with the Royal Naval Volunteer Reserve (Motor Boat Reserve) stationed at Dún Laoghaire Naval Base when he died at the age of 22 on the 29th of July 1918. It is stated in the cemetery records that he was married but no mention of his wife or address was listed in the interment entry.

Bell was buried in grave 90 N1 South-West on the 3rd of August where his army number appears on the military headstone.

Christopher Beresford (service number 31228) was a private with the 6th Battalion of the Royal Dublin Fusiliers. He died aged 22 on the 6th of August 1919 and was buried on the 11th of August in grave 63 J3 North. He was the son of Mrs Sarah Beresford of 59 Lower Clanbrassil Street, Dublin who also signed her son's remains into the cemetery on the day of the burial. His small marble headstone, which was densely covered with ivy, is situated in the upper North section.

Thomas Christopher Blake (service number 1906375) served as an aircraftman 2nd class with the Royal Air Force - Volunteer Reserve based in England. Thomas died when he was 18 years old, after he was knocked down by a car on the 30th of September 1945 while serving during the war. He was the son of Patrick and Mary Blake of 29 Dominick Street, Dún Laoghaire where members of his family still live in this street. Thomas was buried on the 4th of October in grave 14 Z St Itas which also contains the remains of his parents. His military headstone takes pride of place in the centre of two similar stones, where the names of his parents are inscribed.

J. S. Blissett (service number 5592) was a private in the 2nd/7th Battalion of the Sherwood Foresters (Notts and Derby Regiment). Plot number 85 T1 South-West. (See chapter on 1916 Rising)

William Breen (service number 13024359) served as a private with the British Army's Pioneer Corps. He died at the age of 44 on the 26th of August 1941 and was buried in 74 C4 upper North on the 29th of August. William was married to Margaret Breen and they lived at 39 St Oliver Bond House in the Dublin Liberties. His occupation is listed in the interment records as a labourer which was the traditional work carried out by the Pioneer Corps. His mother and father, Gerald and Honora included the following words on his military headstone, which is located in the upper North section.

'In loving memory of our dear William, Jesus, Mercy!
Mary and Joseph pray for him'

John Brennan (service number 24999) was a private with the 5th Battalion Royal Dublin Fusiliers. He died at the age 26 on the 1st of February 1918 and was buried in grave 10 P2 West on the 7th of February. He was the son of Mrs Ellen Brennan of 51 Bride Street, Dublin. John's military headstone is positioned in the centre of the West section, 10 plots in from the pathway which divides the West and the North.

Andrew Breslin was a ship's master with the Merchant Navy and was based on board the M.V. *Teasel* at Cardiff Wales. He was aged 37 when he died on the 12th of January 1941 and his remains were buried in grave 24 R St Itas on the 16th of January. Andrew was the husband of Kathleen Breslin of 7 Amiens Street, Dublin. She died on the 18th of December 1985. The following inscription was added to the military headstone on his grave which is located in the centre of St Itas.

'In loving memory of Andrew.
Sadly missed by his wife and children.
Thy will be done'

Montague Bernard Browne was a Second Lieutenant with the 2nd/8th Battalion, Sherwood Foresters (Notts and Derby Regiment). Plot number 85 T1 South-West. (See chapter on 1916 Rising)

Reginald Patrick Buckley (service number 2725770) was serving as a Guardsman with the 5th Battalion, Irish Guards He was aged 18 when he died on the 2nd of May 1945. Reginald was the son of Denis and Elizabeth Buckley, of 67 Lower Beechwood Avenue, Ranelagh. His grave lies under a young yew tree which is just off the pathway in the centre of the West section where it is marked by a military headstone. He was buried in grave number 40 S2 West on the 9th of May. The crest of the Irish Guards which is on the memorial consists of an eight-pointed star of the Order of St Patrick. At the centre of the crest is a shamrock with a crown on each leaf. Around the shamrock are the words '*Quis Separabit MDCCLXXX111*' which translate to 'Who will separate us 1783'. The date signifies the formation of the Order of St Patrick in 1783.

William Byrne (service number 7043411) served as a Fusilier with the 6th Battalion, Royal Inniskilling Fusiliers. William died aged 27 on the 21st of November 1940 and was buried in grave 8 T2 West on the 25th of November. He was the son of John and Mary Byrne of 72 Bow Lane, James's Street, Dublin. The grave is marked by a military headstone and is positioned a few graves in front of the 1916 plot. At some point his family added three extra words to the bottom of the headstone '*Thy kingdom come*' The regiment's crest on the headstone consists of a three-towered castle flying the cross of St George and is surrounded by shamrock. There is a crown above this and the regiments name below.

Matthew Campbell (service number 2607C) served as a seaman / petty officer aboard H.M. Yacht *Mera* with the Royal Naval Reserve. He died on the 19th of May 1916 at the age of 40 and was buried in grave 17 K2 West on the 22nd of May. Matthew was married to Catherine Campbell and the couple lived with their family at 17 St Mary's Street, Dún Laoghaire. A heart shaped marble plaque that rests on the grave states that Catherine died on the 14th of February 1955. On the bottom of the military headstone is included the details of their daughter Elizabeth who died in 1931 aged 24. The grave is positioned in the centre of the West section, directly in from the Republican Plot.

Charles J. Canning (service number 3173) was a Corporal in the 2nd Battalion, *Leinster* Regiment. He was 25 years of age when he died on the 16th of October 1918. Charles Canning served in the British army under the name Charles Cullen. This was a quite common practice by those who did not want their real identities to be known or who were too young to enlist and so signed up under fictitious names. Today his name appears on the Church of Ireland's 'Mariners Roll of Honour' in the town of Dún Laoghaire. Charles was the son of Sarah and Charles Canning of 38 Merville Place, Dún Laoghaire. He was buried on the 18th of October in the Canning family plot 86 M1 South-West, which is located at the far right hand side of the section. The inscription on the large marble headstone states that '*Charlie*' died '*from illness contracted on active service*' '*He did his duty*'

Brothers James Cash, (service number 11074) & John Cash (service number WR/318897) both died while serving during the First World War. James was a drummer with the 2nd Battalion of the Royal Dublin Fusiliers. He died on the 7th of November 1918 aged 22 years. John served as a sapper with the Royal Engineers (The term 'sapper' is the Royal Engineers equivalent of a private). He was discharged from the army due to injuries received while on active service but died of these same injuries on the 21st of February 1919 at the age of 33.

James lived with his father Denis Cash at the family home in 4 Sandwith Court, Dublin. John on the other hand was married and lived with his wife and family at 8 South Gloucester Street, Dublin.

Headstones of brothers John and James Cash

The families had the extremely difficult task of burying the two brothers less than four months apart, James on the 11th of November 1918 and John on the 23rd of February 1919. Their grave is located at 41 J3 near the centre of the upper North and has two military headstones. When I visited there for the first time, I noticed that a Christmas wreath was lying between the two memorials. Clearly someone still comes to pay their respects to the brothers.

Richard Archibald Cathie was a commander in the Royal Navy. He was aged 66 and lived with his wife Annie at Corrig House in Dalkey He died on the 20th of March 1918 and was buried on the 23rd of March in grave 82 F1 South-West. The memorial is a small granite plinth stone and surrounds, on which a short inscription is weather worn and very difficult to read. The plot is located on the pathway roughly three quarters of the way along the centre of the South-West section.

Christopher Connolly (service number G/1524) served as a private with the 3rd Battalion of the Royal Munster Fusiliers. He was married to Elizabeth Connolly of 35 South Gloucester Street, Dublin, the home they both shared. He was discharged from the British army and must have succumbed to injuries he received during active service. He died at the age 36 on the 21st of November 1919 and was buried in 75 T3 North on the 24th of November. The grave is located in the upper North just off the main walkway and is marked by a military headstone and surround, with the following inscription included:

'Also his son Patrick died in January 1918,
sacred heart of Jesus have mercy on them.
Also his dear wife Elisabeth, died 6th October 1965'

His memorial is engraved with the regimental crest of the Royal Munster Fusiliers which consists of an old type hand grenade and Bengal Tiger.

Michael Connolly (service number 16493) was a private with the 4th Battalion, Royal Dublin Fusiliers and was married to Mary Connolly of 48 Patrick Street, Dún Laoghaire. Michael died aged 48 on Christmas Day, the 25th of December 1917 and was buried on the 27th of December in grave 12 M1 West. The grave is positioned roughly half way along the main walkway between the North and West and 12 plots in to the left. There is a military headstone marking his grave.

Joseph Connor (service number 1904) served as a gunner with the Royal Field Artillery 295th Brigade. A gunner is the equivalent of private in the R.F.A. He lived locally at 40 Sarsfield Street, Sallynoggin with his mother Mary. Joseph chose to enlist under the surname of Murphy while with the British Army. He died at the age of 27 on the 25th of February 1917 and was buried in grave 23 O1 West on the 28th of February. His grave is located in the centre of the West section and is marked by a military headstone.

Denis Crimmins (service number SS/9473) served as an ordinary seaman with the Royal Navy, stationed on board HMS *Vivid*. He was single and lived with his parents Thomas and Margaret Crimmins at 3 Annaville Avenue, Newtown Park, Blackrock. Denis died at the age of 19 on the 21st of February 1920 and was buried in grave 50 H West on the 24th of February. The military headstone on his grave states that he died on the 21st of May, but the cemetery interment records and the family headstone show that he died on the 21st of February. The inscription on the family headstone also states that his mother died the following year.

Michael J. Cullen (service number 27207) was a lance-corporal with the Royal Dublin Fusiliers. He was the son of Mrs Ellen Cullen of 3 Salthill Place, Dún Laoghaire. Michael died at the age of 23 on the 4th of November 1919 and was buried in grave 6 B2 West on the 6th of November. His grave is positioned just off the main pathway between the West and North and is marked with a military headstone.

Fr. James Gerard Curran (service number 211517) was a chaplain 4th class with the Royal Army Chaplains Department. He died suddenly in London on the 4th of May 1944, at the age of 37 James Curran was better known as 'Gerry' to his friends and had worked as a newspaper journalist before entering the priesthood. He was a keen boxing enthusiast and even accompanied the Irish Amateur Boxing team to the Golden Gloves competition in Chicago in 1935. James was ordained in 1938 and three years later volunteered to serve as a chaplain in England for the duration of the war.

Fr. James Curran was buried 1P West which is in the Community Plot of The Holy Ghost Fathers on the 9th of May. The interment records show that his address was given as Holy Ghost College, Kimmage. The Holy Ghost plot can be found just past the Consecration Cross at the start of the West section. He was survived by his parents who lived at St Kevin's, Esplanade, Bray, Co Wicklow.

Frederick Christian Dietrichsen was a captain with the 2nd/7th Battalion, Sherwood Foresters (Notts and Derby Regiment). Plot number 66 K2 South. (See chapter on 1916 Rising)

Headstone of Henry Doran

Henry Doran (service number 25600) served with the Northumberland Fusiliers as a private. He was the son of Mrs Mary Doran of 4 King Street, Mitchelstown, Co Cork. Henry died on the 15th of May 1920 in the Meath Hospital, Blackrock of injuries he received during action. He was aged 22 and was buried on the 17th of May in grave 43 J West. A military headstone marks the spot where he was buried at the far end of the West section. The regimental crest on the memorial depicts St George on horseback killing a dragon which is encircled by the regiment's name. The following words have been added to the bottom of the memorial:

'Died of wounds,
Greater love no man hath
than to die for his friends'

Herbert Richard Dowse (service number 1542071) served as a flight sergeant with the Royal Air Force, Volunteer Reserve. He was better known as 'Dick' and lived at the family home 5 Ardbrugh Villas, Dalkey with his parents Herbert and Florence, at the time he was their only surviving son. His name is listed along with that of his brother, Arthur, on the War Memorial of the Holy Trinity Church, Killiney. His brother was killed while in battle in the skies over Germany the previous year.

Herbert died as a result of an accident in England on the 22nd of October 1944. Herbert was only 22 years old and his remains were buried in grave 14 P St Nessans on the 26th of October. The grave is located near the funeral gate in St Nessan's section. The headstone on the Dowse family grave represents a marble scroll and has the following words inscribed about Herbert:

'Sergeant Pilot Herbert Richard (Dick) R.A.F.V.R.,
Killed on active service in England
22nd October 1944 – aged 22 years. Per ardua ad astra'

The Latin phrase at the end is the motto of the R.A.F. and translates into 'Through Struggles to the Stars'

Daniel Doyle (service number 19310) was a private, serving with the 8th Battalion, Royal Dublin Fusiliers. He was married and lived at 35 Powerscourt, Mount Street, Dublin. Daniel was 36 when he died on the 12th of October 1918. He was buried on the 16th of October in grave 22 P4 West. Daniel's grave is marked with a military headstone and is located to the furthest edge of the West section. The grave faces into the West section as it was once positioned along the old back wall of the cemetery, before this was pulled down to facilitate the opening of St Brigid's.

Arthur Doyle (service number 30960) served as a private with the Royal Irish Fusiliers. He was a 25 year old single man who lived at 27 Glasthule Buildings in Dún Laoghaire. He died on the 14th of February

1919 and was buried in grave 30 N West on the 16th of February. His grave is in the centre LHS of the West section and is marked by a military headstone. The crest of the R.I.F. is inscribed into the memorial and depicts an old type grenade, burning beneath a crown. The regiment's motto is '*Faugh a Ballagh*' which is Gaelic for 'Clear the way'.

Hugh Dunne (service number 12774) served as a private with the 6th Battalion, Royal Dublin Fusiliers. He was aged 28 and lived at 72 York Road, Dún Laoghaire. Huge died on the 27th of January 1915 and was buried in grave 59 T3 North on the 30th of January. The grave is positioned in the centre of the upper North section and is marked by a military headstone.

John (Jack) Eager (service number 6405010) had served as a private with the 8th Battalion, Royal Sussex Regiment. He was the son of William and Eiscalla Eager and was married to Annie Eager of 12 Sarsfield Street, Sallynoggin. Jack died at the age of 38 on the 12th of August 1940 and was buried in grave 3 G St Fintan's on the 15th of August. His daughter Mary died in 2002 and a new polished granite headstone was placed on the grave. The inscription states that his wife Annie died in 1957. The grave is positioned near the front of St Fintan's, not far in from the main drive.

Charles Robert Easton (service number 209335) was an able seaman in the Royal Navy and was stationed aboard HMS *Vivid.*

He died at home, aged 35, on the 16th of June 1918. Charles was married to a Mary Easton from Dún Laoghaire. His remains were buried in grave 20 N2 West on the 18th of June. His grave is roughly a third of the way along the West section and in the centre. It is marked with a military headstone with the following words added to the bottom:

'Died at his residence 3 Library Road Kingstown'

Alfred Ellis (service number 21735) served as a private with the 5th Battalion, Royal Dublin Fusiliers. Plot number 85 S1 South-West. (See chapter on 1916 Rising)

Peter Ennis (service number 10404) was a Private with the 1st Battalion, Scots Guards. Plot number 25 V2 West. (See chapter on 1916 Rising)

Thomas Henry Evans (service number 239495) was a petty officer with the Royal Navy on board H.M. Submarine *H12.* He was married to Edith Evans of 119 Belvedere Road, Ipswich. He died on the 6th of June 1918 and his body was taken into Dún Laoghaire on board H.M. S. *Vulcan*. He was 26 years of age when he was buried in grave 76 S South-West on the 10th of June. There is a military headstone marking the grave which is positioned in the centre of the section.

James Farrell (service number 1837131) was an aircraftman 2nd class with the Royal Air Force, Volunteer Reserve. James was a son of Patrick and Annie Farrell from 27 Eden Villas, Glasthule. James died at Halton R.A.F. base in Buckinghamshire, England on the 21st of September 1944 aged 23 years. His remains were taken home to Ireland and buried in grave 12 F St Fintan's on the 26th of September. The grave with its military headstone is located not far in from the cemetery's main drive. At the bottom of the marker is the inscription of his parents.

'Patrick Farrell died June 28th 1939.
Annie Farrell died Dec 16th 1949'

Patrick Farrell, (service number 1127676) served as a private with the Pioneer Corps. He was married to Annie Farrell of 99 Lower Georges Street, Dún Laoghaire but sadly had lost her six years previously when she died aged 29. Patrick died on active service at the Longmaster military camp, Stratford-upon-Avon, Warwickshire on the 30th of May 1944. He was buried in grave 71 D St Mary's on the 5th of June at the age of 38. Patrick has a military headstone on his grave which is located close to the intersection with St Patrick's section. His brother included the following words into the inscription:

'In loving memory of my dear brother Patrick'

Thomas Laurence Christopher Farrell (service number 1797500) was an aircraftman 2nd Class with the Royal Air Force, Volunteer Reserve. He was the son of Lawrence and Mary Farrell, 323 Clogher Road, Dolphins Barn, Dublin. Thomas died at the age of 23 on the 8th of June 1945. His remains were interred in plot 24 F1 St Fintan's on the 11th of June. His grave which is in the centre of St Fintan's is marked by a military headstone and has the following words added:

'In loving memory of
my son Thomas Laurence Christopher,
deeply regretted by family'

The inscription also states that his father and mother were interred with Thomas in 1962 and 1966 respectively.

Kevin Finbarr Fidgeon (service number 7047368) served as a fusilier with the 5th Battalion, Royal Irish Fusiliers. He was a single son of Edward and Margaret Fidgeon of 39 Glasthule Road, Dún Laoghaire. Kevin died aged 20 on the 24th of November 1941 and was buried on the 26th of November in grave 72 H St Mary's. At some point the military headstone which once stood on Kevin's grave was removed and placed lying flat on the grave. This was to facilitate the erection of a new monument, which included the names of his mother, father, sister, and of Kevin's. The grave is a few plots in front of that of Patrick Farrell.

Daniel Patrick Finn (service number 393610) served as a rifleman with the 9th Battalion, London Regiment (Queen Victoria's Rifles). He was married to Elizabeth Finn of 1 Pembroke Cottages, Donnybrook in Dublin. Daniel died at the age of 36, on the 30th of April 1918, and was buried in grave 103 F1 North on the 5th of May. The plot is located in the lower North section and has a military headstone. The names of Rosie Finn, Elizabeth Finn and Gus Finn are also included on the marker.

James Fitzpatrick (service number S4/093939) was a private with the Royal Army Service Corps. He was married to Beatrice Fitzpatrick of 17 Upper Baggot Street, Dublin. He died on the 30th of April 1920 aged 39 and was buried in grave 57 I West on the 3rd of May. James was discharged from the Army after receiving injuries during active service. Beatrice, who signed his body into the cemetery on the day of the burial, died on the 1st of July 1936 and was laid to rest beside her husband. The grave is marked by a marble headstone and is located at the far end of the West section close to the Special Memorials.

Michael William Fitzpatrick (service number 13122156) served as a private with the Pioneer Corps and was aged 16 ½. Michael lied in order to join the British Army and was put to work as a labourer with the Pioneer Corps. Like so many young men at the time Michael traveled to England in search of work but ended up in the army. He lived at 35K Pearse House, Pearse Street, Dublin and died on the 24th of March 1945.

The remains of the young soldier were interred in grave 88 G3 North on the 28th of March. There is a military headstone marking the grave, which is in the upper North section. The crest of his regiment which is on each soldier's military stone depicts a rifle crossed with a pick and shovel and the motto '*Labor omnia vincit*' which translates as 'Labour conquers all things'.

Percy Gerald Gilbert was a cadet in the Royal Military Academy and was training to be an officer while studying at the Royal Military Colleges, Sandhurst and Woolwich. Percy lived at 11 Eaton Square, Monkstown and died while home on leave on the 19th of November 1918. The remains of the 19 year old were interred in grave 35 U1 South on the 21st of November. His grave is located, hidden under a yew tree at the far end of the South section. The gothic marble headstone was so overgrown that I had to cut away at the ivy in order to see the following inscription:

'In loving memory of Percy Gerald Gilbert,
late Cadet R.M.A. Woolwich,
only son of Lt. Col. & Mrs Gilbert.
Born Umballa India 26. Nov. 1899.
Died Monkstown 19. Nov. 1918.'

Ernest Edward Glorney served as a lieutenant with the Royal Flying Corps. The corps preceded the Royal Air Force as Britain's fighter planes squadron. Ernest lived at the family home Allington in Ballsbridge before going on to hold a position in the Straits Settlement of the British East India Company in South East Asia. He resigned his position at the outbreak of the First World War in order to join the Royal Flying Corps and had only qualified as a flying officer the previous September.

Ernest died as a result of an air accident on the 25th of October 1916 while returning with a new plane to the front. He was aged 28 and his remains were interred in the family vault (Glorney vault) on the 31st of October. The vault is located directly up from the cemetery offices on the main walkway between the upper North and South-West sections.

Robert Kingston Gray

Robert Kingston Gray (service number 105154) was a corporal with the 191st Training Squadron, Royal Air Force. He was the eldest son of John and Catherine Gray, who lived at 2 Crofton Avenue, Dún Laoghaire. Robert was a former member of the 'Kingstown Co Boys Brigade'. At the outbreak of war in 1914 he joined the Royal Irish Horse and was transferred to the R.A.F. in 1917. 'Bob' as he was known to family and friends contracted influenza while based at Upwood Aerodrome in

Ramsey, Cambridgeshire. An influenza pandemic had swept across the globe during this time, causing the deaths of millions. Robert died of pneumonia on the 2nd of November 1918 aged 25. His remains were returned to Ireland and interred in grave 12 M2 South, which is on the pathway directly behind the cemetery office, on the 6th of November. His parents, who are also interred with Bob, erected a large marble memorial on his grave with the following inscription.

'He now is sweetly sleeping, his sprit rests with thee.
And though thy saints are weeping, their song is victory'

Charles Edward Harman served as a colonel with the Royal Dublin Fusiliers. He was the husband of Edith Harman who lived at 23 Hogarth Road, Kensington, London and served as a Brigadier General while in India during 1903. He died at the age of 59 while stationed in Co Cork and would become the first of 102 British service personnel to be buried in this cemetery between 1915 and 1947.

His remains were interred in grave 69 J South-West on the 9th of January 1915. The grave is roughly situated between the Glorney vault and the Protestant Chapel and his memorial consists of three marble tiers with cross and the following inscription:

'In loving memory of Colonel C.E. Harman, The Connaught Rangers,
youngest son of J. Bower Harman Great Marlow, Buck's.
Born in London June 10 1855,
Died while serving his King and Country at Buttevant,
Jan. 5. 1915. R.I.P.'

Peter Harold (service number C/KX64992) served as a petty officer stoker with the Royal Navy aboard HMS *Folkestone*. He was the son of James and Sarah Harold of 278 Merrion Road, Dublin. Peter died on the 8th of June 1943, aged 37, and his remains were interred on the 10th of June in grave 38 V St Itas, located to the centre RHS of the section and has a family headstone which is made of limestone.

Captain Stanley Hollinshead served as a master on board SS *Alexandra* and was based in Liverpool with the merchant navy. The merchant navy was responsible for the shipment of materials during war and as Britain and Ireland were islands this was the only way any real supplies could me delivered between both countries.

Stanley was married to Violet Hollinshead and the couple lived at Carradale, 9 Martello Avenue, Dún Laoghaire. He served with the Merchant Navy throughout World War I, during which his ship was torpedoed. A native of Limerick, Stanley began working with the Irish Lights Service in 1919 as a junior. He showed great skill at his job and went on to command the *Ierne*, *Isolde* and eventually the *Alexandra.*

Having been ill for a number of months, Stanley died on the 4th of December 1943, aged 51. His remains were interred on the 7th of December in grave 15 H St Nessans, located 8 plots in from the main drive and marked by a military headstone. The cemetery records list Stanley as a captain with the merchant navy. The crest on the memorial consists of the letters MN surrounded by rope beneath a crown.

Arthur Walter Patrick Inman served as colonel during the war with the Royal Army Medical Corps. He was 65 years old and was married to Constance Inman. He died at home with his wife by his side at 10 Eglington Park, Dún Laoghaire on the 17th of June 1920. His remains were buried in grave 61 N1 South-West on the 19th of June.

While researching Arthur's burial location, I discovered that the military headstone was placed on the wrong grave. The CWG memorial was in fact in an entirely different section, the lower North at plot 25 N1. Arthur's actual burial plot has a family headstone consisting of granite cross with pedestal. The inscription cannot be read as it is very badly worn and the entire grave is covered by a granite slab.

Arthur Henry Jeffries was a Wireless Operator with the Mercantile Marine, stationed on board SS *Leinster*. Plot number 90 T1 South-West. (See chapter on *Sea Disasters*)

William James Victor Johns (service number J/43841) served as a leading boatman with H.M. Coastguard, based at the Dún Laoghaire Coast Guard Station. William was aged 21 when he died on the 20th of December 1920. He lived at 2 North Street, Tywardreath, Cornwall with his wife Kathleen, the couple had only married in June 1919.

William is listed with the Commonwealth War Graves Commission as being buried in the cemetery, but his burial location is unknown. The commission placed a 'Special Memorial' along with those of three other servicemen, against the boundary wall between the South-West and West sections. During research, I found William's burial location at 96 P1 South-West. His remains were interred here on the 23rd of December 1920 after his wife Kathleen signed them into the cemetery earlier that day. The grave is not far from where the Special Memorials are placed and close to those of other British service men in the far right hand corner of the section. I have met with a representative of the C.W.G.C. and the commission hopes to have a headstone placed on William's grave in the near future. His name appears beside those of fellow military personnel on the Tywardreath Village War Memorial.

William Joyce (service number 23040) was a lance-corporal with the 7th Battalion the Royal Inniskilling Fusiliers. He had transferred to (336822) Labour Corps but by 1918 he was discharged from the army after receiving injuries during active service. He died at Our Lady of Lourdes Hospital, Rochestown Avenue, Dún Laoghaire on the 26th of December 1918. William was aged 21 and was the son of Mrs Margaret Joyce of Cashel, Recess, Co Galway. His remains were interred on the 28th of December in grave 38 W2 West. His plot is located on a pathway in the middle of the section and is marked by a military headstone. The memorial states that he died on the 28th of December but the cemetery record states that he died on 26th and that he was buried on the 28th.

James Joseph Kelly (service number 4865620) was a private with the 6th Battalion, Leicestershire Regiment. He was 54 and single and was the son of John and Bridget Kelly of 6 Sallynoggin Villas, Dún Laoghaire. James died on the 14th of February 1941 while on active service at Ashby, St Legers near Rugby, England. James's remains were interred in grave 43 C1 West on the 17th of February. There is no mention on the family headstone of his military involvement and he is listed as a 'bricklayer' in the cemetery records. The memorial on the grave is marble with a granite plinth and also mentions his parents and his sister Emily. The plot is situated in the centre of the West section.

Michael Kelly (service number 2987) served as a rifleman with the Royal Irish Rifles. The title 'rifleman' is equivalent to that of a private in other regiments. He was age 20 and was the son of Mrs E. Kelly of 6 Temple Road, Blackrock Co Dublin. Michael died on the 5th of August 1916 and was buried in grave 45 O1 North on the 8th of August. The grave is marked with a military headstone and is located just off the pathway between the lower North and the Registrar's house.

Patrick Kelly (service number 7558) was a rifleman with the 15th Battalion, Royal Irish Rifles. He was married and lived at 31 Dodder View, Dublin.Patrick was transferred to (SN. 329767 Pte) Labour Corps before his death on the 23rd of November 1919. He was aged 31 when buried on the 26th of November in grave 40 H West. The grave can be located by taking the 2nd pathway after the Republican Plot and eight graves into the RHS, where it is marked by a military headstone.

Herbert Colles Kennedy (service number 269041) was a gunner with the 2B Res. Brigade, Royal Field Artillery (Cadet Officers Training Corps, Dublin) He was the son of the Very Rev. Dean H. B. Kennedy, BD of The Mariner's Church Rectory, Dún Laoghaire. Herbert was born at Naas, Co Kildare and studied at St Columba's College, Dublin before leaving there in 1913. He went on to Dublin University where he became a member of the college's Officer Training

Corps. His name is listed on the school's 1914 - 1918 Memorial Plaque. He died on the 15th of October 1918 at Brighton Military Hospital England after contracting sceptic pneumonia through blood poisoning. He was buried at the age of 19 on the 18th of October in the family plot at 61 O South-West. His grave is marked by a granite cross and plinths, which is close to the Protestant Chapel.

James Kennedy (service number 20159) was a private with the 1st Battalion, Royal Dublin Fusiliers. He was married to Ellen Kennedy of 49 Montpelier Parade, Monkstown, Co Dublin. James died aged 32 (his headstone states 37) on the 9th of April 1919. His remains were interred in grave 20 Q West on the 12th of April. His burial plot is directly along the pathway at the Republican Plot which turns in towards the section and is marked by a military headstone.

Charles Kenny (service number 7347) served as a private with the 7th Battalion, Royal Dublin Fusiliers. He lived with his parents, Catherine and John, at Kilmacud Road, Stillorgan, both of whom are now buried with him. Charles died aged 30 on the 17th of February 1918 and was buried in grave 5 R West on the 20th of February. The burial plot is located just off the pathway between the West and North sections.

William Lang (service number 3290) was a private with the 2nd/7th Battalion, Sherwood Foresters (Notts and Derby Regiment). He is believed to be buried in this cemetery. (See chapter on 1916 Rising)

Martin Lawlor (service number 10307) was a private with the 1st Battalion, Royal Dublin Fusiliers. He was single and lived with his family at 6 Turners Cottages, Ballsbridge. Martin died at the age of 26 on the 13th of March 1917 and was buried in grave 94 Q3 North on the 16th of March. His grave is marked by a military headstone and is located in the upper North. The crest on the headstone bears an old type grenade, burning, with a picture of a tiger and elephant, above the regiment's name. The regiment was created in 1881 after the amalgamation of two regiments based in India and the East India Company, which is why the animals are represented on the crest.

Robert Ernest Lee served as a captain with the Royal Army Medical Corps during the First World War. Plot number 47 D1 South.
(See chapter on Sea Disasters)

Richard Lennon (service number M2/033377) was a corporal with the Motor Transport Company, Royal Army Service Corps. He was single and lived at 67 Williamstown, Blackrock. His occupation is listed in the cemetery records as a chauffeur, which was most likely his role within the Corps. Richard was 39 when he died on the 25th of September 1917. His remains were interred in grave 90 E1 North on the 26th of September. The burial plot is located in the centre of the lower North and is marked by a military headstone.

George Crow Lugton (service number 10306DA) was a deckhand in the Royal Navy, stationed on HMS *Boadicea II*. He was the son of John and Eliza Lugton of 14 Custom House Square, Dunbar, East Lothian, Scotland. George died, aged 32, on the 10th of October 1918 and was buried in grave 91 N1 South-West. His burial date was not recorded in the interment book. His grave is marked by a military headstone and is in the far right-hand corner of the section. The headstone bears the crest of the Royal Navy which consists of a rope and anchor.

John Lynch (service number 13009951) served as a private with the army's Pioneer Corps and is listed as a 'laborer' in the cemetery interment records. He was married to Mary Lynch and the couple lived at 4 St Audoen's Terrace, High Street, Dublin.

John died, aged 38, on the 1st of November 1946 and was buried on the 4th of November in grave 57 Z3 West. His burial plot is close to the wall at the far right-hand corner of the section and is marked by a military headstone. A small heart-shaped marble plaque on the grave contains the names of his parents Patrick and Mary who are also buried here.

Patrick Lynch (service number M/279006) served as a private with the 615th Motor Transport Company, Royal Army Service Corps. He was listed in the cemetery interment records as a chauffeur, and was married to Mary Teresa Lynch, who lived at 11 Brighton Terrace, Foxrock, Co Dublin.

Patrick died at the age of 44 on the 16th of May 1918, and was buried on the 19th of May in grave 28 U West. The burial plot, which is situated near the centre of the section, has a military marker, as well as being inscribed with the following '*Mollie Lynch died on the 18th of April 1920 age 22*'. I believe this to be his daughter.

Patrick Lynch headstone

Thomas Maher (service number 16540) was a private with the 2nd Battalion, Royal Irish Regiment. Although 26 is the age referred to on the headstone, Thomas was only 21 when he died on the 30th of October 1918. He was single and lived at 4 Georges Place, Blackrock. His remains were interred in grave 22 E1 West on the 3rd of November. Thomas's burial plot is situated in from the Republican Plot towards the centre and a few graves into the left. His grave is marked by a military headstone.

Cyril John Massy (service number 365941) was a lieutenant with the 8th King's Royal Irish Hussars, Royal Armoured Corps. He was the son of the Hon. Francis and Eveline Massy who lived at Ardline, Newtownpark Avenue, Blackrock. Cyril is the last of those buried in Dean's Grange Cemetery that is commemorated by the Commonwealth War Graves Commission.

Cyril was aged 21 when he died on the 7th of April 1947. His remains were interred in grave 71 V1 South-West on the 11th of April. The burial plot is located at the far left hand corner of the section and has two headstones at either end of the grave. At the foot of the grave is Cyril's military memorial and facing it at the head is a family memorial with the names of his mother and grandmother. The grave lies directly before that of Thomas McLoughlin.

James Bernard McCall was an able seaman stationed on SS *Duchess of Bedford* (London) with the Merchant Navy. He was single and was the son of Richard and Mary McCall, 4 North Wall, Dublin Bernard died at the age of 26 on the 1st of February 1944 and his remains were interred in grave 3 M St Mary's on the 3rd of February. There is a military headstone on the grave, but at some point the face of it was covered by new piece of limestone that now included the names and dates of Bernard and his parents, but no mention of his military involvement. It is located at the top left hand side of the section beside the gravedigger's compound.

Thomas Alexander McLoughlin (service number 1697680) was an aircraftman 2nd class with the Royal Air Force Volunteer Reserve. He was originally from Belfast and was stationed in England during the war. He died at R.A.F. Chedburgh, in St Edmunds, Suffolk on the 2nd of July 1943.

Thomas was aged 19 and was buried in grave 71 X1 South-West on 7 July. His burial plot is located two graves beyond that of Cyril Massey, close to the top left hand side of the South-West. The headstone is made of granite and has a marble face with the crest of the R.A.F. carved into the top. The following is inscribed underneath:

'In loving memory of our youngest and dearly beloved son
L.A.C. (Leading Air Craftsman) Thomas A. McLoughlin R.A.F.
Killed on active service 2nd July 1943, aged 19.
The sun went down while it was yet day'

Thomas is buried with both of his parents and their grave is located directly in front of Cyril Massy.

Jessie McTaggart (service number 14390) was a member of the Women's Royal Air Force. She was the daughter of William and Anna McTaggert and lived at 56 Pembroke Road, Dublin. Jessie is the only female member of the British forces buried in Dean's Grange who is listed on the C.W.G.C Roll of Honour.

Jessie died after a short illness in the Meath Hospital Dublin on the 21st of January 1919. She was aged 24 years and her remains were interred in grave 83 Z South-West on the 23rd of January. The burial plot is situated in the centre of the section and is marked by a large Celtic cross memorial and Jessie's military headstone which sits at the foot of the grave. The R.A.F. crest is at the top of her memorial and consists of the motto '*Per ardua ad astra*' in a circle beneath a crown and an eagle in flight at the front.

Alfred P. Miller (service number 34784) was a sergeant in the Signalling Company 15th Battalion, Royal Field Artillery. He was single and lived with his brother at Tivoli Lodge, York Road, Dún Laoghaire. Both his father and grandfather served in the British Army.

Alfred died at home aged 30 on the 24th of June 1920. His remains were interred in grave 30 B2 West on the 26th of June. The burial plot is sheltered under a yew tree near the centre of the West section and is marked by a military headstone. On the headstones regimental crest the phrase '*Ubique, Quo Fas Et Gloria Ducunt*' is carved and means 'Everywhere, Where right and glory lead' these words surround an artillery cannon which are based beneath a crown.

John Mulhern (service number 5797) served as a rifleman with the 3rd Battalion, Royal Irish Rifles. Plot number 49 L West. (See chapter on 1916 Rising)

Joseph Murphy (service number 9584) was a private with the 4th Battalion, Royal Dublin Fusiliers. He was aged 19 and lived with his mother at 5 Pilot Cottages, Blackrock. Joseph enrolled into the army under the name of Kinsella. He died on the 7th of January 1916 and was buried in grave 28 N1 North on the 12th of January. His plot is situated at the lower end of the North, near to the registrar's house and is marked by a military headstone.

Robert Anthony Murphy headstone

Robert Anthony Murphy (service number 1909938) served as an aircraftman 2nd class in the Royal Air Force Volunteer Reserve.

He was 17 years of age and was the son of James and Elizabeth Murphy of 133 Leighlin Road, Kimmage Dublin. Robert died on the 2nd of January 1947 and his remains were buried in grave 34 E4 North on the 4th of January. The burial plot, situated in the upper North is marked by a military headstone, which states that Robert died at the age of 19. His parents added the following words to his memorial: '*Memory is the only thing that grief can call its own*'

Martin Murray (service number T/33489) was a Driver with the Army Service Corps and was attached to the Royal Army Medical Corps. He died on the 30th of June 1918 in Our Lady of Lourdes Hospital on Rochestown Avenue from injuries he received during active service. Martin was aged 22 and was buried in grave 23 XX North on the 3rd of July. The grave is located at the top of the lower North a few graves in from the pathway opposite the Catholic Chapel.

Richard O'Brien (service number 13030499) was a private with the British Army's Corps of Military Police. He was married to Annie O'Brien and the couple lived at 10 Lombard Street, Dublin. Richard died age 28 on the 27th of August 1945 and his remains were interred in grave 29 K1 St Fintan's on the 1st of September. The grave is located near the centre of the section and is marked by a military headstone. There is also a marble plaque that commemorates his wife Annie who died in 1982. Annie had the following passage inscribed on Richard's headstone:

'In memory of my beloved husband,
died at Queen Alexandra's Military Hospital England'

James Phoenix (service number T/40420) served as a corporal/driver with the 3rd Reserves, Horse Transport Depot, Royal Army Service Corps. He was 25 years old and married to Bridget Phoenix of Galloping Green, Stillorgan, Co Dublin. James died on the 27th of April 1918 and was buried in 20 Y2 West on the 2nd of May. His plot is on the pathway that leads in from the Republican Plot and is roughly two thirds along the way. There is a military headstone marking the spot and some family ornaments, which indicate that someone still visits this grave.

Patrick Prendergast (service number 90834) was a private with the Royal Defense Corps Reserves Depot. The Royal Defense Corps was the equivalent of the home guard and consisted of personnel that were unsuited to overseas service. He was single and originally from 56 Strand Street, Tralee, Co Kerry. Patrick died in the nearby Our Lady of Lourdes Hospital, Rochestown Avenue on the 27th of May 1920. His remains were conveyed to Dean's Grange Cemetery the following morning and interred in grave 127 R North. The grave is marked by a military headstone and is situated at the bottom end of the lower North towards its centre.

Gerard Philip Regan (service number 281030) was a lieutenant with the Pioneer Corps. He was 36 years of age and single and lived at 5 Temple Road, Blackrock. Gerard died in hospital on the 7th of December 1944. His remains were interred in the cemetery at 147 C St Patrick's on the 9th of December. His headstone is made of granite and the inscription is in a very poor state. It is located about one third along the section and three plots from where it joins the North section. I was able to make out the inscription which reads as follows:

'In loving memory of Gerard Philip Regan, Barrister at Law
Blackrock Co Dublin. Lieut Pioneer Corps British Army.
Wounded in battle Normandy June 1944, Died 7th December 1944
at Netherleigh Military Hospital Belfast.'

Edward Reilly (service number 19230) served as a gunner (School of Gunnery) with the Royal Garrison Artillery. He was married to Helen Reilly and the couple lived at 19 Railway Road, Dalkey. Edward served in South Africa during the Boer War between 1899 and 1902. He died on the 13th of May 1917 aged 38. His remains were interred in grave 10 X2 West on the 15th of May. The burial plot is marked by a family headstone of a marble cross and base resting on a granite plinth. It is located at the near corner of the section close to St Brigid's.

James Reilly (service number 215472) was an able seaman stationed on board HMS *Salmon* with the Royal Navy. He was 32 years old and lived at 14 Upper Oriel Street, Dublin. James died on the 24th of September 1918 and his remains were buried in grave 136 I North on the 26th of September. His graved is marked by a military headstone and is situated in the lower North close to the turnstile gate.

Arthur Ferdinand Richards (service number 98195) was a second lieutenant with the army's Intelligence Corps. He was married to Maureen Richards of Coombe Lane, Wimbledon, England. Arthur received a Diploma in Modern Languages from Heidelberg University in Germany and would have been immediately accepted into the Intelligence Corps of the British forces, especially during WWII. He died at the age of 65, in Our Lady of Lourdes Hospital on the 24th of November 1940. His remains were conveyed to the cemetery for burial on the 26th of November and interred in 103 A North. The plot is marked by a granite cross with base and is situated only a few yards beyond the pathway that leads from the turnstile gate, near the plot of Count John McCormack (see Notable People).

David Roberts, (service number J/41628) was an able seaman aboard H.M. Trawler 'Aracari' with the Royal Navy. Robert was aged 27 when he died on the 25th of March 1919. He was married to Catherine Roberts of 35 St Salvador Street, Dundee, Scotland. His remains were removed from the Naval Base in Dún Laoghaire and interred in Dean's Grange Cemetery on the 28th of March in grave 93 R1 South-West. There is a military headstone marking the plot and is located at the far right hand side of the section.

Henry Rooke was a Skipper aboard HM Trawler *Dragon* IIwith the Royal Naval Reserve. He was the husband of Mary Elizabeth Rooke of 35 Dartmouth Street in the Welsh town of Milford Haven. Henry was 28 years old and was living at 5 Mulgrave Street in Dún Laoghaire at the time of his death. He died on the 8th of October 1918 and was buried in 91 K1 South-West on the 10th of October.
His grave is located in the far right hand corner of the South-West and is marked by a military headstone. The following words were inscribed on the bottom of the memorial:

'Far too far from sight and speech,
but not too far for thoughts to reach'

Joseph Ryan (service number T1/1357) was a driver with the 120th Company, Royal Army Service Corps. He was the husband of Winifred Ryan of 73 Glasthule Buildings, Sandycove, Co Dublin. Joseph died

Joseph Ryan headstone

while he was on active service at Aldershot England on the 19th of May 1915 aged 28. His remains were brought home and interred in 34 G3 West on the 24th of May.

The plot is marked by a military headstone and is positioned in the far right-hand centre of the section close to a large Monterey cypress tree. The crest at the top of the headstone includes the motto '*Honi soit qui mal y pense*' which loosely translates to 'Shame upon him who thinks evil of it'

Michael Saul (service number 1485) served as a private with the South Irish Horse regiment. He was single and the son of Mrs Mary Saul of 10 Martello Avenue, Sandycove. Before the war Michael worked at the Royal St George Yacht Club in Dún Laoghaire and today his name appears on the clubs Roll of Honour plaque for those who died during the First World War. He was 18 years of age when he died on the 9th of April 1916. His remains were buried in grave 17 N West on the 12th of April.

Charles Saunders (service number 4953) was a Private with the 2nd/6th Battalion, South Staffordshire Regiment. Plot number 85 S1 South-West. (See chapter on *1916 Rising*)

David Mansfield Saunders served as a lieutenant-colonel with the Royal Army Medical Corps. He was married to Margaret Saunders of Kilcolman, Glenageary, Dún Laoghaire. David died at home aged 56 on the 2nd of December 1918. His remains were interred in grave 93 B

North on the 4th of December. The plot in which David is interred is situated on the pathway that leads from the turnstile gate up alongside the North section. It is roughly half way along the path and on the right hand side. The memorial is marble and consists of a cross on four plinths, which is in a triple plot.

Robert Saunders (service number 12105DA) served as a Deck Hand while stationed with H.M.T. *Grecian Empire* with the Royal Naval Reserve. Robert was single and the son of Elizabeth Saunders of 71 Park Cottages, Pigeon House Road, Ringsend, Dublin. Robert died at the age of 20 on the 24th of February 1917. His remains were buried in grave 11 T2 West on the 26th of February. The plot which is marked with a military headstone is located at the beginning of the section near to the middle.

William Scott was a captain with the Army Veterinary Corps. William was born in Tipperary and moved to Australia when in his early twenties. While in Australia Scott became the principal veterinary surgeon of the NSW Defense Forces and took part in the Boer War.

In 1896 he married Emily White, a horse breeder, but his new bride died tragically the following year after moving to Scotland. William had become a well known horse breeder and won many titles throughout the late 1800's and early 1900's at meetings in Australia, England and Ireland. His most famous was a stallion named 'Abercorn', which was regarded as one of the finest racing horses of its era and made its owner financially secure when he was put to stud. Another horse was a colt named 'Ca Ira II' which won the Leopardstown Grand Prize in 1900.

Not long after the death of his wife, William moved back to Ireland and settled at Shanganagh Grove in Killiney. At the outbreak of the First World War, he joined the Remount Department supplying horses for the army.

On the 11th of November 1917, William Scott died at his residence aged 58. His remains were interred in grave 61 U South-West on the

14th of November. The memorial which marks his plot is very ornate, depicting a statue of an angel kneeling to place flowers at his grave. The angel is carrying a harp in her left hand and bears a mournful expression upon its face. The statue is perched on a large granite rock with William's name and the date of his passing etched on the front. It is located directly to the South of the Protestant chapel.

Alfred William Smith (service number 1191/TS) was an engineman on board HMS *Boadicea II* with the Royal Naval Reserve. His last place of residence was listed as the Dún Laoghaire Naval Base. Alfred died on the 9th of October 1918 and was buried on the 12th of October in grave 91 L1 South-West. The plot is located at the far right hand corner of the section and is marked with a military headstone. The crest on the headstone is simply a rope and anchor, used by both the Royal Navy and Reserve.

Edward George Stevens (service number M/2702) was a wireless telegraphist with the Royal Navy stationed aboard HMS *Boadicea II.* He was the son of Lily and the late George Stevens of 67 St Leonard's Road, Rodwell, Weymouth, England. Edward was single and after his death his body was removed from the Naval Base in Dún Laoghaire for burial. Edward died of pneumonia aged 27 on the 26th of October 1918. His remains were interred in 92 N1 South-West on the 28th of October. The plot is located at the far right hand corner of the section and is marked with a military headstone.

Joseph Valentine Tierney (service number 73108) was a corporal with the Royal Engineers, stationed at the Signal Department in Fenny Stratford near Milton Keynes. He was the eldest son of Mary and Patrick Tierney of Milltown Lodge, Co Dublin and before the war was remembered for skill on the rugby field for St Mary's College in Rathmines.

Joseph had only joined his regiment in September 1915 and was immediately sent out to France. It was in France two months later, while acting as a dispatch rider that he had a terrible accident and was sent back to the UK. Joseph died of his injuries at the British Red Cross Hospital in Glasgow on the 5th of January 1916. He was aged 24 and was buried in grave 109 H1 North on the 8th of January.

The burial plot is located on a grass area opposite the cemetery office. This is a double plot with a large marble family headstone and at the foot of the grave is Joseph's military headstone. There is a further inscription at the base of the marker for his brother William, which reads as follows:

'Also Cpl. W (Walter) .L. Tierney M.M. Royal Engineers
Died 12th January 1923 age 28'

There is no reference to Walter on the Roll of Honour list of the Commonwealth War Graves Commission as he died working as a merchant after the war and not while on active service.

Ernest George Tozer (service number 3204/SD) was a deckhand stationed on board H.M. Motor Lighter *233* with the Royal Naval Reserve. He was single and the son of Samuel and Sarah Tozer of 8 Hill Street, Ogmore Vale, Bridgend in Wales. He was aged 21 when he died on the 20th of October 1918. His remains were removed from the Naval Base in Dún Laoghaire and brought for burial to Dean's Grange Cemetery on the 22nd of October.

Ernest's remains were interred in grave 91 S1 South-West. His grave which is marked by a military headstone is located in the far right hand corner of the South-West section. '*A flower that once was mine*' is also inscribed at the base of the memorial.

Michael Tyrell (service number 3/5697) served as a corporal with the 3rd Battalion, Royal Irish Rifles. He was married to Bridget Tyrell of Talbot Road, Killiney, Co Dublin. Michael died on the 10th of November 1918 aged 42 and was buried in 56 G4 North on the 14th of November. His grave is located in the upper North section opposite the Glorney vault. The plot bears a military headstone with the R.I.R regimental crest carved into the top.

Henry Tyrrell was a quartermaster with the Mercantile Marine and worked on board the RMS '*Leinster*'. Plot number 92 K1 North. (See chapter on *Sea Disasters*)

Peter Patrick Walsh (service number 1494549) was a corporal with the Royal Air Force, Volunteer Reserve. He was married to Bridget Walsh of 18 Beaumont Road, Whitehall, Dublin. Peter was aged 39 when he died on the 10th of July 1943. His remains were interred in plot 20 A1 St Itas on the 13th of July. The grave has a family headstone made of red granite and Peter's military stone is placed lying flat down in the centre. The plot is located near the centre of St Itas section.

Sean Wheeler headstone

Sean Wheeler (service number 1103602) served as a gunner with the 3rd Reserve Medium Regiment of the Royal Artillery, after enlisting in the army under the name of Michael. He was the son of Charles and Alicia Wheeler of George's Place Dún Laoghaire. Sean died at 18 years of age on the 13th of July 1941. His remains were interred in plot 11 K2 West on the 17th of July. The following words were added to the base of his military headstone.

'No morning dawns
nor evening falls
but I remember him'

Sir William Ireland de Courcy Wheeler
Courtesy of the Royal College of Surgeons in Ireland

Sir William Ireland de Courcy Wheeler was a surgeon with the Royal Navy and lived at 32 Merrion Square, Dublin and Robertstown, Co Kildare with his wife Elsie (nee. Shaw of Dunfermline) the couple were married in January 1909. He was regarded as one of the finest surgeons in Ireland and the U.K. and was honored by various medical institutions around the world. The following is a list of his medical titles, M.D. B.Ch. B.A.O. F.R.C.S.I. F.A.C.S. (Hon.) M.Ch. (Hon.) University of Egypt.

Billy, as he was known, was aged 64 and he held various positions in hospitals around Dublin, chiefly the Mercer's Hospital. He was a past President of the Royal College of Surgeons Ireland and was author of several publications on Medicine and Surgery. In 1914 he lent his fully equipped private hospital to the Red Cross and St Johns Ambulance for the treatment of wounded British officers. For this and other public duties during the First World War William was twice mentioned in army dispatches and in 1919 was knighted.

At the outbreak of WWII he became consulting surgeon to the Admiralty with the rank of Surgeon Rear Admiral and was posted to Aberdeen in Scotland. His last address was listed in the cemetery records as The Royal Northern Club in Aberdeen. It was here on 11 September 1943, when preparing for dinner at the exclusive club that William took very ill and died.

His remains were cremated and six months after his death they were interred in grave 34 C St Nessans on the 16th of March 1944. The memorial on his grave is a granite Celtic cross on a plinth and the inscription states that he died on active service and was with the force from 1939 until his death in 1943. The plot is located three graves in off the main drive.

William Williams (service number K/14097) was a stoker 1st class stationed aboard HMS *Boadicea II* with the Royal Navy. He was married but was stationed at the Naval Base in Dún Laoghaire during the First World War. William is one of those included on the special memorials that are located between the South-West and West sections. During research I found that his interment details were not listed into the cemetery records until February 1919. His grave is now officially recorded at 9F P1 South-West.

He was aged 26 when he died on the 26th of October 1918. His remains were interred in the grave, which is situated in the far right corner of the section, on the 30th of October. As with William Johns the C.W.G.C. hope to have a headstone placed on William's grave in the near future.

Walter Wright was serving as an assistant cook with the Mercantile Marine Reserve, and was stationed with H.M. Yacht *Helga*. He was aged 27 and was the son of Sarah and the late Archibald Wright of Law View, West Kilbride, Ayrshire in Scotland. Walter died on the 19th of October 1918 and was buried within the cemetery. It is not known where exactly he is buried and his military headstone is included with the other special memorial, between the South-West and West.

Arthur William Young (service number 2123/T) served as a chief stoker with the Royal Naval Reserve, stationed on board HMS *Hyderabad*. He was the single son of William and Rachel Young of South Bank, Yorkshire in England. Arthur died on the 7th of February 1919 aged 34 and was buried in grave 24 Q2 South. There is no record of Arthur's burial in the cemetery interment books and therefore I was not able to establish that he was in fact buried in the above plot. The only person listed as interred in this grave is that of a baby boy buried in 1891 and no other is recorded. This does not mean he was not buried here as human error could easily have led to his burial been omitted from the records. The grave bears Arthur's military headstone and is located directly behind the offices.

Irish War of Independence & Civil War

'...whereas at the threshold of a new era in history the Irish electorate has in the General Election of December 1918, seized the first occasion to declare by an overwhelming majority its firm allegiance to the Irish Republic. Now therefore, we; the elected Representatives of the ancient Irish people in National Parliament assembled, do in the name of the Irish nation, ratify the establishment of the Irish Republic and pledge ourselves and our people to make this declaration effective by every means at our command.'

The above text is taken from the Declaration of Independence, which was adopted by Dáil Éireann on the 21st of January 1919.

Dean's Grange Cemetery, like many others around the country, has buried within its grounds people who died during both the War of Independence and the Civil War. The town of Dún Laoghaire and surrounding areas saw their share of fighting during these disturbing times and many engagements in the area resulted in injuries and several deaths.

The following pages include IRA Volunteers, young men from all walks of life who met their deaths under various conditions of those conflicts. There are also other young men, National Soldiers of the Free State who in the latter Civil War fought against their old comrades in the IRA. The deaths were not restricted to those directly involved in the fighting and, in many instances, civilians would also pay the ultimate price. The saddest of these is that of a young girl shot while playing outside her house. All the civilians were simply in the wrong place at the wrong time.

There are spies shot by the IRA because of their involvement and alleged involvement with the British authorities.

It seems largely as a result of most wars that it is those that have taken part in the fighting and who died that are commemorated and civilians who have also suffered are mainly forgotten. This chapter represents the times in which they lived and died, and presents a broader overview. It also commemorates them together.

Alan Bell - 26th March 1920

In March 1920, the Intelligence Department of the IRA, famously led by Michael Collins, undertook the execution of one of its biggest enemies, the new Resident Magistrate of Dublin. The Magistrate Alan Bell, had recently been transferred to Dublin from Belfast in order to take up his new position in Dublin Castle, which for hundreds of years was the epicentre of British rule in Ireland. Alan Bell was chosen by his superiors in the Castle to investigate the recent attempt on the life of Lord French, the Lord Lieutenant of Ireland. But there was another reason that Bell was brought to Dublin and that was also to locate the IRA's hidden finances and those who donated money to the fund.

Bell, who was originally from Co Offaly, was aged 62 and a long time serving member of the British Secret Service. Hidden beneath this seemingly ordinary looking man was an even darker side. Alan Bell had held a long and distinguished portfolio of involvement as covert agent in British intelligence operations in Ireland and as agent provocateur in incidents notably centred on the Land League and Home Rule.

He was chiefly responsible for the arrest of the American author Henry George during the latter's Land League visit to the west of

Ireland in 1882 and for which the British Government embarrassingly had to apologise to the United States. It was also discovered during the 'Pigott Forgeries Case' in 1889 that Bell was a Secret Service agent handling a forger named Richard Pigott. The secret service tried to discredit Charles Stewart Parnell and Home Rule, by producing forged letters that supposedly showed that C.S. Parnell supported the Phoenix Park killings in 1882. The forger, Pigott was an old friend of Parnell's, and was working as a journalist with the Times newspaper. He confessed in court that he was bribed by the Secret Service to fake the letters.

By 1920, Bell was sanctioned with another job and now wanted to know every bank client who contributed to the Dáil Funds and National Loan and where this money was kept. On the 1st of March 1920, Bell ordered all banks in Dublin to appear at the Police Courts so that his officials could scrutinise their records. Within days, Bell recovered a staggering £18,000 from different accounts belonging to the republican movement. Collins wasn't going to allow Mr Bell to locate much more of the funds and sent his men to find the Resident Magistrate and eliminate him.

Collins knew that Bell made his way into Dublin each morning by tram, but didn't know at what time or even Bell's description. It took the intelligence unit a few days, but they soon found their man. At the time, Alan Bell was living with his wife at number 19 Belgrave Square in Monkstown and each morning was left to the tram at Monkstown Church by an armed detective. He would travel alone on the tram until he was met by another detective when it reached his stop in Dublin city.

On the 26th of March 1920, four members of the Dublin IRA unit boarded the tram in which Alan Bell was already seated. The unit waited their time as they had previously chosen the stop at Sandymount Avenue as the location at which they would remove Bell from the tram. On reaching the stop three of the men approached Bell, who was seated to the front nearest the door and took him by force from the tram. Although he was armed, Bell didn't get the chance to draw his revolver and as he was forced on to the footpath just adjacent the doorway of the tram, the fourth member of the unit following behind removed a gun from his pocket and fired three shots into the back of the Magistrate. The IRA unit quickly made their escape and disappeared along streets in the surrounding area as the shocked passengers were only coming to realise what had happened.

In this operation, the IRA succeeded in removing one of Dublin Castle's best agents and thwarted any further efforts by the British authorities at finding the Dáil Funds. The killing sent shockwaves through the Houses of Parliament in London, and the British Prime minister, Andrew Bonar Law, raised the killing in the House of Commons.

The remains of Alan Bell were brought to Dean's Grange Cemetery on the 29th of March and interred in a double plot, which is located in the South-West section. The plot has a marble Celtic cross headstone and plinth and is located a few graves behind the Glorney Vault. The plinth is inscribed with the following inscription:

'To the proud and beloved memory of Alan Bell,
who died in Dublin on the 26th of March 1920, aged 62.
Duty well done through many years even unto death.'
'Thou will keep him in perfect peace, whose mind is stayed on thee,
because he trusteth in thee. Isaiah 26.3.'
'Also his wife Ellen Sherrif Bell, rest and assurance forever'

Annie O'Neill - 13th November 1920

It is always a sorrowful thing for any parent to lose a child and much worse when the child is taken from them because of someone else's actions. This was the case when a girl of 8 years was shot as she played on the pathway outside her home on the afternoon of Saturday, the 13th of November 1920.

Moments before she was shot, a few young men were standing at the corner of Charlemont Street and Avenue when a military lorry carrying soldiers and a with two officers came speeding over the canal bridge. The two vehicles skidded to a halt near to where the men were standing. Some of the young men were frightened and took off running up the Avenue, quickly followed by two of the officers who by now had drawn their revolvers and were calling on the men to 'halt'. The lorry carrying the soldiers also drew up alongside the entrance to the Avenue and it was reported that some shots were fired in the direction of the fleeing men. The officers in pursuit also fired a number of shots but never managed to hit their intended targets.

At the same time, Kathleen O'Neill was in her house at number 22 Charlemount Avenue when she heard the gunfire from outside. Realising that her young daughter, Annie, was outside playing, Kathleen ran out on to the street, picked up her daughter, and carried her into the house. It was while inside that Kathleen noticed Annie could not stand and then suddenly blood began to pour from the girl's mouth. Little Annie was shot straight through the chest from one of the officer's guns. As her mother began to panic and scream with fear, a neighbour ran into the house and took the dying child from her mother's arms and wrapped her in a shawl. Annie's body was limp in the neighbour's arms as she walked over to the soldiers and told them that they shot the girl. She was rushed to hospital but sadly, died on the way. One of the British officer who first left the car, took full responsibly for Annie's death. But there can be no justification for the shooting of a child, especially when the excuse was trying to shoot a young man in the back for merely running away.

On the morning of the 17th of November little Annie's remains were taken to Dean's Grange Cemetery and buried beside those of her father who had died the previous August. A photograph which appeared in the *Irish Independent* on the 18th of November portrayed a grim picture of Annie's small white coffin being carried on the shoulders of four male relatives while on their way to the cemetery. The grave which is located in the centre of the upper North section and, like many in this area, bears no headstone and is unnoticeable in the surrounding ground.

Vol. John Hickie - 14th December 1920

It was well over a year after the start of the War of Independence when the Irish Republican Army undertook a new strategy of using guerrilla tactics in an attempt to overthrow British rule in Ireland. This new strategy was in stark contrast to that of the uprising used by their predecessors during Easter 1916.

On a cold winter's night on the 12th of December 1920, an Irish Republican Army Volunteer, John Hickie, was on manoeuvres near Merrion Gates, on the outskirts of south Dublin city, when he was mortally wounded by a gun shot. Very little is known about the circumstances surrounding the shooting of the 25 year old, except that he was found with a wound to his abdomen after locals heard shots in the area at around seven o'clock in the evening. The newspapers reported that John was shot and 'wounded under mysterious circumstances' near the railway crossing half-way between Dún Laoghaire and the city.

Hickie was taken by ambulance to Baggot Street Hospital where he underwent an emergency operation on the wound to his stomach. The operation proved futile and John eventually died two days later on Tuesday, the 14th of December. His address was listed in the cemetery records as 142 Cross Avenue in Dún Laoghaire town and that he was employed as a Draper's Assistant.

John was a member of the local IRA unit and would have been on active service at this time during the Tan War. The rail track between Dún Laoghaire and Dublin city was an ideal way for any unit to move around as the trains would have finished at that hour of the night and the roads would be considered too risky to travel.

The only explanation to his shooting is that he himself, or another member of a unit, could have discharged their gun by accident, tripping on a rail track or sleeper with the obvious dire results. British military forces had not engaged in fighting at this location that night, so this scenario could be ruled out.

John's remains were conveyed to Dean's Grange Cemetery for burial in the West section. The grave is located just in off the footpath between the West and South-West sections, roughly 20 spaces along from the Republican Plot. Today there is no headstone on this man's grave, which I feel is an indictment of past governments who have failed to acknowledge such people, by at least marking their final resting place. The same can be said about Andrew Cunningham who died during the 1916 Rising and who also has no gravestone.

Peter Graham - 21st May 1921

Peter Graham

Peter Graham was a 23 year old man from Dún Laoghaire who worked as a porter at the Pavilion Gardens in the town. Peter was working at the gardens up until 5pm on the 21st of May 1921, when he left work to meet his girlfriend. He was due back at his post later that evening at 8pm; but never arrived.

Just before six o'clock on the same day, a car containing five men stopped beside a set of gates which led into a field opposite St Matthias Church (C. of I,) Ballybrack, which is about three miles from Dún Laoghaire. One of the men in the car was Peter Graham and the others were Volunteers of the Dún Laoghaire IRA. As the car stopped, Peter was told to get out and was marched through the gate to a point at the far end of the field. At this point Peter was told to say his final prayers and as he knelt there in the grass, one of the Volunteers fired a number of shots into the back of his head. The three men then quickly returned to their waiting car and drove off in the direction of Killiney Avenue and back towards the town. Later that evening when military soldiers arrived, local residents pointed them to where they discovered Peter's body lying within a clump of gorse bushes at the top end of the field close to the Golf Links. Attached to his body was a note on which the following statement was written:

'Convicted Spy tried and found guilty by the I.R.A.'

For some reason Peter was shot a total of five times in the head, which was a very excessive punishment even in those times. In one of his clasped hands they also found that he was holding a sacred picture. It is not known why the IRA had found Peter to be a 'spy' but on his headstone there is a mention of his brother Christy, who was lost at sea while serving with the Royal Navy in 1919. Whether it was this that brought Peter into confrontation with the local IRA, or something totally different, he paid for it with his life.

The remains of Peter Graham were buried beside those of his father, young sister and brother, who were all previously interred in the cemetery. Today the inscription on the six foot high limestone tablet memorial reads as follows:

Erected by Annie Graham
Barrett Street, Dún Laoghaire
In memory of her beloved husband
Patrick died 9th May 1918 aged 56 years
Also her children
Elizabeth died 4th Oct 1914 aged 15
Christy lost at sea 7th Feb 1919 aged 23
Peter killed 21st May 1921 aged 23
Patrick Leo died 27th April 1925 aged 21
R.I.P.

Vol. Edward Dorins - 25th May 1921

In early 1921, the leadership within the Army Council of the IRA decided that a major military operation was necessary against the Crown Forces in Ireland. This was believed to be for two main reasons: firstly, to boost the morale of Volunteers around the country who had seen very little advancement of the struggle and secondly, to strike back with a heavy blow against the British forces, who had inflicted heavy casualties on the Volunteers along with large scale arrests of their personnel. A final decision was taken to destroy the Custom House in Dublin city. This building was the epicentre of the Irish civil administration, holding government departments as well as the tax files for Ireland and local government records and its destruction would hamper the administrations ability to govern.

On the 25th of May 1921, small groups of IRA Volunteers began entering the Custom House at various entrances around the building and, as planned, quickly gathered up all staff and visitors into the main hall, where they were held at gun point. The IRA Volunteers had also taken with them cans of paraffin oil, with which they began to douse every floor of the building. When the signal was given, they set the Custom House alight. At the same time, another Volunteer unit held up the fire station at Tara Street, on the opposite side of the River Liffey from the Custom House. This action was taken in order to prevent the fire brigade from reaching the building and extinguishing the fire.

The idea for holding the people in the main hall was to enable the Volunteers to make their escape at the same time as their hostages, mingling with them as they dispersed along the city streets. The whole operation was planned to last no more than 25 minutes and to arouse as little suspicion as possible. But unfortunately suspicion was raised and IRA units stationed outside the Custom House were soon engaging in gun battles with British Forces as the building began to burn.

In the end, a total of five Volunteers, two civilians and a small number of British soldiers died as a result of the operation. One of the Volunteers who died was named Edward Dorins. Edward who lived on Church Road, only a short distance away from the Custom House was a member of the 2nd Battalion Dublin Brigade. He was on guard along with other Volunteers near Talbot Street when they were confronted by a group of Black and Tans. A gun battle ensued in which Edward was fatally wounded and he died where he lay on the street moments later. Edward was 22 years old and was working as a plumber in the city. Three days after he was killed, Edward's remains were laid to rest in the upper North section of Dean's Grange Cemetery. The grave is situated only a few plots along from the Consecration Cross and inward from the pathway. The inscription on the white marble headstone that marks Edwards's grave reads:

'Erected in loving memory of my son, Edward Dorins, Late I.R.A.
Killed in action at the Custom House May 25th 1921.
Also of his dear Father, Thomas Dorins,
died 19th January 1940 aged 76 years.'

The IRA achieved their objective that day and the Custom House was totally gutted. Many Irish newspapers were to condemn the burning of such a 'fine architectural building' and calling the operation 'senseless and wanton'. In return the IRA Army Council replied to the newspapers by accusing the same journalists of deliberately remaining silent when many homes, shops and town halls were destroyed around the country under the direction of the British government. As well as loss of life, the building held many government files which where indeed another great loss to future generations.

Michael 'Paddy' Smyth - 29th May 1921

At the far end of the West section, there is a large limestone memorial in the design of a Celtic cross and which bears the following inscription:

'Erected by his mother,
in loving memory of
Michael J. Smyth (Paddy) Donnybrook.
Who was shot by Black & Tans
at 17 Anglesea St, Dublin.
29th May 1921 aged 19½ years.'

Paddy Smyth was working as a grocer's assistant at a shop behind what is currently the Central Bank, in Dublin's city centre. It was around ten o'clock in the evening when Paddy was standing outside the shop, enjoying the evening air. He was waiting for the owner to close up for the night when suddenly without warning, a shot was fired from a passing military lorry.

As the lorry drove slowly along Dame Street, one of the occupants took aim and shot at the young man as he stood in the doorway. The bullet hit Patrick in the arm and passed on right through to his chest. He was taken to Jervis Street Hospital, where he died soon after arriving. If the Black and Tans in the lorry had taken the shot believing Paddy to be an IRA Volunteer, then surely they would have stopped, but they didn't, and he became just another pot-shot for the force. It was never discovered where the lorry came from or where it went after the shooting, and no constable was ever charged with the killing of the young man.

On the 1st of June, the broken-hearted mother of Paddy Smyth interred her son's remains in Dean's Grange cemetery. The headstone is the only one I have come across where the inscription gives a reference to the Black and Tans. The fact that these words were inscribed into the memorial shows the hurt caused to this woman. The ordinary people of Ireland had come to despise this vile auxiliary police force, the role of which was to protect citizens, not to kill them. Paddy's mother has literally set the Black and Tans cruel actions in stone for future generations to see.

Vol. Thomas Murphy - 30th May 1921

Vol. Thomas Murphy

There once stood a hotel in the centre of Foxrock Village to the left hand side of what is now the entrance to a Pitch & Putt course. The Foxrock Hotel was situated at the village cross roads, then adjacent to the entrance of the Dublin & South Eastern Railway station (since terminated) and it was here that a well known local republican named Thomas Murphy lived with his mother and sisters. Thomas worked part time as a porter with the railway company and those who knew him in the locality described him as a very popular young man. He also drove a motor car for Sir Horace Plunkett who lived nearby in Leopardstown. On the morning of the 30th of May 1921, Thomas was due to rise early and meet the Mail Boat on its arrival at Dún Laoghaire Harbour, but before he could, was shot and mortally wounded as he lay in bed.

At approximately three o'clock in the morning, a group of five masked men entered the hotel through the front door and quietly made their way to Thomas's room. The men then burst through the bedroom door, waking the startled man from his sleep. One of the intruders asked if he was Thomas Murphy and on his affirmative answer shot the young man in the head. On hearing the shooting, his mother and sisters rushed into his room and found Thomas in a collapsed state and bleeding from his wound. The local priest and a doctor were summoned but there was little that could be done, only to administer the last rites to the dying man. By seven o'clock that morning, Thomas succumbed to his injuries and died where he lay in bed.

The probability is that Thomas was shot by Black & Tans as a reprisal for the shooting of a local policeman, Albert Skeats at the rear of the RIC barracks in Cabinteely two weeks previously. Skeats had been in a coma since the shooting but died in Steevens hospital Dublin two days before the killing of Murphy.

The man who, in fact, shot Skeats was another local republican named Leo Murphy (not related), who was also a good friend of Thomas. Both men had taken part in numerous attacks on military patrols and police barracks in the area. In one such attack, the two men posed as British Army officers and, along with a driver, drove towards Cabinteely barracks in a car. As the car came up outside the entrance to the barracks, the Volunteers opened fire on troops stationed outside.

Thomas was a strong, fit-looking young man with fair hair, who always dressed well. He was a drummer with a local pipe band and appeared with them at meetings around the country.

Thomas Murphy's remains were brought for burial to Dean's Grange Cemetery on the 1st of June 1921 and interred in a grave at the centre of the West section. His memorial consists of a beautifully carved granite headstone and surrounds, which has the following inscription:

'In Loving Memory of Corporal Thomas Murphy,
E. Coy 1st Batt. No2 Brigade S.E. Division, I.R.A.
Who died for Ireland 31st May 1921, aged 22 years.
Go ndeunaid dia trocaire ap a anam.
Erected by his brothers in arms.'

The Gaelic text within the inscription loosely translates to asking God to have mercy on his soul.

Although the inscription on his headstone states that he died on the 31st of May, Thomas actually died on the morning of the 30th of May which is recorded in the cemetery's Interment records and also in newspapers which carried the story of his killing.

John Joseph Healy - 12th June 1921

On the evening of the 12th of June 1921, a convoy of military vehicles containing British soldiers was travelling in the direction of Dublin City, after collecting mail in Dún Laoghaire. The five vehicles, which included two cars, a tender and another two lorries were travelling at speed along the main road into the city and were directly opposite Merrion Railway Gates when they came under attack. Their ambushers consisted of 11 Volunteers of the IRA's Dublin Brigade ASU (Active Service Unit), B Company, 6th Battalion who were hidden behind the wall of an asylum for the blind on Merrion Road.

The Volunteers lobbed a number of bombs at the convoy as it passed their position, bringing it to a stop. Immediately following the explosions they fired a barrage of shots from rifles and revolvers as the soldiers began exiting their Lorries.

The tender then swung around and entered the gates of the asylum and began returning fire on the Volunteers position. The unit only managed to fire a few dozen rounds before been forced to retreat. Neither side in the ambush reported having had any casualties but two civilians had died during the fighting.

The victims were both male and neither had played any part in the fight. The first was a night watchman named James Brophy, who was shot at his residence. The other was a local insurance agent named John Healy. Mr Healy had just left a grocer's shop in Merrion village, about 200 meters on the Dublin side of Merrion Gates. As the fighting broke out, John tried to take cover in the grounds of Elm Park on the far side of the street. He stooped down low as he ran, but just as he got to the other side, he was hit in the head by a bullet and fell face down on the pathway. When the fighting ceased, passers-by rushed to John's aid but found that he was dead. A local priest administered the last rites and shortly afterwards he was removed to the Royal City of Dublin Hospital.

As well as being an insurance agent, John Healy was previously elected a member of the Blackrock Urban Council. He was aged 48 and lived locally with his family at 12 Carysfort Avenue.

It was reported in the Irish Times that a court of military inquiry found that John's death was

'through misadventure, and that he died from gun shot wounds, inflected by forces of the Crown in the execution of their duty during a conflict with armed rebels'

On the 15th of February 1921 the funeral procession of John Healy made its way to Dean's Grange Cemetery for burial. Many people attended the service including family and friends, but also members of staff from the Blackrock Urban Council and sympathetic locals for whom John worked tirelessly over the years. Described as a constitutional nationalist, John Healy was laid to rest in the lower North. The grave is positioned not far from the gate lodge and only a few plots inward from the main walk at the edge of the trees. There is a small granite headstone which states that his wife, three daughters who died in infancy, his son, and daughter-in-law are all now buried with him. Inscribed in Gaelic at the bottom of the headstone are the words '*Suaimhneas Siorai*' which mean Rest in Peace.

Vol. James McIntosh - 22nd June 1921

The Royal Marine Hotel is situated in the centre of Dún Laoghaire town, overlooking Dublin Bay. During 1921, the hotel was the most predominant building visible to passengers arriving by boat into the local harbour.

For many years before and during the war of Independence, the hotel was used to billet British Army officers and Auxiliaries who otherwise would not have been accommodated in the local barracks. The IRA would have made use of any opportunity to attack crown forces and on the night of the 19th of June 1921 the local unit took such a chance.

The unit received information that British officers, who they had targeted for execution, were at the Hotel, and Volunteers quickly planned an attack. The unit had not taken the precaution of sending a scout into the hotel to survey the situation first and when they entered the main lobby of the Royal Marine they came face to face with their targets. Guns were drawn from both sides and a small fight erupted as civilians ran for cover. The man leading the IRA, James McIntosh, was only able to discharge one round from his revolver before it jammed and was himself injured by returning fire from the Auxiliaries.

McIntosh managed to retreat from the hotel but due to his wounds only made it as far as Marine Road, just outside the main gates of the hotel where he collapsed. James was then taken the short distance to St Michael's Hospital but died there the following Wednesday on the 22nd of June.

McIntosh was working as a butcher in Dún Laoghaire and was renting a room on Patrick Street. The 34 year old, who was originally from Portlaoise, had been living in the area for a number of years and was well liked in the locality. On the morning of the 26th of June, a large crowd gathered in the centre of the town for the funeral which was held in St Michael's church, situated on the same road opposite where he had collapsed.

As the funeral mass finished and the cortege left the church, it was stopped by a number of British soldiers as the procession turned on to Lower Georges Street. One of their officers approached the hearse and removed the Tricolour flag which was draped over the coffin. It was reported that a young local woman quickly grabbed the flag from the officer's hand and held it behind her back. Incensed by the woman's actions, Black & Tans who accompanied the officer reacted by firing their rifles over the heads of the mourners, sending people running to the safety of the church and side streets. At the same time, another young woman threw herself over the coffin, fearing the soldiers were also going to attack it. The soldiers didn't succeed in stopping the funeral and it proceeded to Dean's Grange Cemetery, where James became the first person to be laid to rest in what was to become the Republican Plot.

In the weeks following his death a truce came into force between the IRA and Britain, but unfortunately, it was a month too late for James.

Roughly 50 years after his death, the Corporation of Dún Laoghaire built a new residential estate to the west of the town. The lands on which these houses were to be built belonged to a woman who had once dated James. She never married and part of her agreement with the Corporation was that the new estate be named 'James McIntosh Park' in honour of the sacrifice that he made for the independence of his country.

Vol. John Jenkins - 4th May 1922

While the truce and negotiations between Dáil Éireann and the British Cabinet were ongoing, Volunteers based around the country were unsure of what the negotiations held in store for them or whether the consequences of any such agreement would stand up to scrutiny.

In the local garrison stationed at the Naval Base in Dún Laoghaire Harbour, a 32 year old member of the IRA named John Jenkins was one such Volunteer. John previously served as a British soldier and gained over ten years experience with that force. It was stated that on the morning of the 4th of May 1922, that John Jenkins accidentally discharged a rifle at the Naval Base, sending a bullet through his skull. He was immediately rushed to the nearby St Michael's Hospital but the doctor on duty there pronounced him dead on arrival. It is hard to believe that a soldier with ten years experience would be able to kill himself with a rifle, but if this was an accident then it would prove to be a costly exercise indeed.

John Jenkins left behind a wife and six children. He lived with his family at their home in St Mary's Cottages in the nearby village of Monkstown. His funeral took place on the morning of the 8th of May with full military honours. The procession was made up of his Comrades from the Naval Base and those from other detachments around South Dublin as well as members of the Na Fianna Scouts and Legion of Ex-Servicemen. A pipe band and fife and drum band led the large procession through the streets of Dún Laoghaire as they played the Dead March. When the cortège reached Dean's Grange Cemetery, John's coffin was laid to rest beside that of James McIntosh in the Republican Plot. As his remains were lowered into the grave John's comrades from the Naval Base fired a volley of shots in salute.

John Bambrick - 30th June 1922

The Anglo-Irish Treaty was signed in London on the 6th of December 1921. It would lead to the creation of an Irish Free State with control over 26 counties, but remaining under the dominion of the British Empire. The Treaty also left six of the counties of Ulster under direct British rule. The decision divided the opinions of the Irish people and its government (Dáil Éireann). Most people reluctantly accepted the Treaty but there were many who saw it as a sell out, and wanted the Treaty voted down at all cost.

Old comrades in the IRA and Dáil Éireann became new enemies on Pro-Treaty or Anti-Treaty sides and so the birth of the Irish nation would start again exactly where it had ended the previous July, with two opposing sides at each others throats.

The harbour area of Dún Laoghaire was the scene of many attacks on the British forces stationed there during the War of Independence. When the Civil War broke out army officers of the Free State realised this as a weak spot within the town and decided to position National soldiers at different locations along the harbours promenade. Their plan failed to deter the Volunteers and the attacks continued, almost on a weekly basis throughout the summer of 1922.

During one such attack the IRA used a car in what can be described as a drive by shooting on National soldiers based in the Coastguard Station. The Volunteers drove at high speed along the front of the station and fired towards the building as they went by. Soldiers inside reacted and returned fire at the occupants of the car as it sped away.

There were no casualties reported, but as in many cases a civilian would pay the price for this attack.

John Bambrick was out walking along the seafront when the shooting began. He didn't have time to take cover during the cross-fire and received a fatal wound to his heart. John, who was aged 56, lived at Avoca Square in the town and worked locally as a labourer. He was unmarried and was buried in the upper North section of the cemetery. The grave is located a few plots from the pathway close to the consecration cross. The grave is not marked by any headstone and is covered by a small cypress conifer tree.

The jury at John's inquest found that his death was due to '… accidental shooting by some person or persons unknown…'

Pte. Patrick Smyth - 7th July 1922

In late June to early July 1922, IRA units in and around the greater Dublin area had suffered great losses both in positions they once held and in mounting casualties. Large numbers of Volunteers directed their attention towards Blessington on the Dublin and Wicklow border, which was still a republican stronghold. Units converged on the town and surrounding areas, setting up camps near outlying roads and buildings.

National soldiers of the Free State Army, at the same time, were slowly making their way from Dublin and the Curragh Camp towards Blessington in order to overthrow the Volunteers. Republicans also held the small village of Brittas which is on the main road into the town from Dublin. In a three pronged advance towards Blessington, a party of National soldiers became embroiled in a fierce gun battle with Volunteers near a house called Brittas Lodge on the 7th of July. Two soldiers of the National Army were shot during this first engagement, one of whom was seriously. injured Patrick Smyth a private in the National Army was the man seriously wounded and he died at the scene soon afterwards. It took another hour of fighting before the

Volunteers in that area finally surrendered. It would be a number of days before the National Army re-captured Blessington. The battle resulted in heavy casualties on both sides.

Pte Smyth belonged to D Company, 1st Battalion, 2nd Dublin Brigade of the Free State Army. He was aged 19 and was from Sarsfield Street, Sallynoggin. His funeral took place on the 11th of July at St Michael's church in Dún Laoghaire. After the service his remains were conveyed to Dean's Grange Cemetery for burial accompanied by a military guard of honour from his Brigade Headquarters in Dún Laoghaire. As Patrick's coffin was lowered into the grave a firing party released a volley of shots above as a mark of respect. There is no headstone upon Patrick's grave today which is located at the very start of the lower North. The plot is beside the grass area in front of the office. The title 'soldier' is recorded in the cemetery's Interment Record beside his name.

Comdt. Reginald Dunne &
Vol. Joseph O'Sullivan - 10th August 1922

As a result of of the Civil War and uncertainty towards the Boundary Commission, which was set up to decide the border between Northern Ireland and the Free State, Loyalists began their own little war in the north-east of the country. By this time the six counties of Northern Ireland were still under British rule but had experienced an accelerated rise in sectarian violence. A pogrom was ongoing by Loyalists and Crown Forces, particularly against Catholics

Comdt. Reginald Dunne

in Belfast and was causing unease amongst Pro-Treaty leaders like Michael Collins. Although his actions were in breach of the Anglo-Irish Treaty, Collins organised small shipments of guns to be sent to Catholic areas of Belfast in order that residents could protect themselves and their communities. This was far from enough as the sectarian violence continued and so another solution was required.

It was believed that the main instigator of these pogroms was Field Marshal Sir Henry Wilson, the Chief of the Imperial General Staff of the British Army who had become Military Advisor to the Northern Parliament under Sir James Craig. Wilson held a passionate hatred of Irish Republicanism and was a staunch supporter of the Orange Order and Unionism as well as an M.P. for North Down. In order to prevent further slaughter of civilians in the six counties it was decided that Field Marshal Wilson would be removed from the equation and his assassination was planned. As Wilson lived in London, the responsibility for this fell to the London Brigade of the IRA and two of its finest members, Joseph O'Sullivan and Reginald Dunne.

Vol. Joseph O'Sullivan

Joseph O'Sullivan, aged 25, was born in London to Irish parents. While only a teenager he joined the British Army's Munster Fusiliers and fought during the First World War. He was discharged from the force after losing his leg below the knee while on active service in Ypres, Belgium. As a civilian, he was employed as a clerk in the Ministry of Labour in Whitehall and became involved with local republican groups and later joined the London Brigade of the IRA in the summer of 1919.

Reginald Dunne was aged 24 and was also born to Irish parents. He joined the British Army's Irish Guards during the First World War and was also wounded during fighting in France. On leaving the Army, he studied to become a teacher. He joined the IRA in 1919, along with O'Sullivan, and later became second-in-command to Sam Maguire.

On the morning of the 22nd of June 1922, Sir Henry Wilson was unveiling a memorial plaque to railway workers who died during WW1. On returning to, his London home in Eaton Place in up-market Knightsbridge that afternoon, Wilson was gunned down on the steps of his house. The Field Marshal was still wearing his full military uniform and sword when he stepped from a taxi-cab outside his home. The two men approached Wilson as he took the first steps to his front door. They opened fire with their Webley revolvers as the aged soldier attempted to remove his sword in defence. Wilson managed to get to his door but the Volunteers made sure he didn't make it any further and ended his life there and then, shooting him a total of nine times.

But disaster was also to strike the two men as they tried to make their escape. A car which had been previously arranged to pick up the men did not arrive and, because of O'Sullivan's disability, their escape would be hard fought. As the two attempted to flee on foot they were pursued by police and members of the public who witnessed the shooting. As their pursuers grew in number the men made vain attempts to keep them back by firing at the police. By the time they reached Ebury Street, about a half mile distance from Eaton Place, the crowd had caught up with Joseph O'Sullivan. Reginald Dunne could easily have made his escape then, but heroically turned back to help his comrade who, by this time, was cornered against railings by the crowd. During Dunne's attempt to protect O'Sullivan, a policeman was shot dead and another three were wounded. In the end, the two men were finally overpowered and the crowd, numbering well over a hundred, almost beat the two to death before they were eventually taken away by the authorities.

The shooting of Wilson sent shockwaves through the British establishment. The King of England cancelled a banquet that was to be held for his son the Prince of Wales. A meeting of the Northern Parliament under James Craig was postponed and armed guards were assigned to all British ministers.

While in custody, Dunne and O'Sullivan gave their names as James Connolly and John O'Brien respectively, but later, during interrogation and torture, their real identities were extracted. The capture of the two men placed Michael Collins in a very precarious situation as a letter found on Dunne mentioned the 'Big Fellow' a nickname commonly used in referring to Collins by his friends.

Back in Dublin, Anti-Treaty forces were occupying the Four Courts (the High Courts of Ireland) since the previous April in opposition to the Anglo-Irish Treaty. Because of the letter found on Dunne, the British Cabinet in London was now putting pressure on Collins to remove these forces from the Courts. Eight days later on the 28th of June 1922, Collins gave in and ordered the Free State Army to attack their old comrades in the Four Courts, ironically using guns and artillery supplied by the British Army. This action was the beginning of the Civil War.

Back in London Dunne and O'Sullivan were awaiting their trial in Brixton Prison, for the murder of Wilson. Leaders from both sides of the fighting in Ireland sent Volunteers to London to determine the feasibility of the men's escape from prison. Scotland Yard received information that the there was a plan to free the men and armed security was stepped up at the prison and the Old Bailey court house, where the men would stand trial. No attempt was made by either side to free the men by force.

The subsequent trial was a farce and the crown judge, Sherman, was hardly able to hide his disgust, saying that he thought 'hanging was too good for them'. The judge denied them their fundamental right to plead not guilty, in order that they might justify their action. Dunne and O'Sullivan were found guilty and on the 18th of July 1922 both men were sentenced to death by hanging.

The following lines are taken from a statement which Reginald Dunne was denied permission to read at the end of the trial:

'...we have both been in the British Army. We both joined
voluntarily for the purpose of taking human life,
in order that the principles of which this country stood should
be upheld and preserved. Those principles, we were told,
were self-determination and the freedom for small nations'

'There is and can be no political liberty in a country where
one political party outrages, oppresses, and intimidates
not only its political opponents, but persons whose religious
opinions differ from those of the party in power.
The same principles for which we shed our blood on the Battle
Field of Europe led us to commit the act we are charged with'

In the weeks before their execution, the men were refused all visits and letters from their families and all appeals to reprieve the death sentence were dismissed. On the morning of the 10th of August 1922 Reginald Dunne and Joseph O'Sullivan were taken from their cells in Wandsworth Prison and escorted the short distance to the scaffolds. The two, who had not seen each other since the trial, exchanged faint smiles of recognition and encouragement when they met for their last brief moments.

Reginald Dunne

'I trust that a Higher Court will consider
the purity of my intentions.'

Joseph O'Sullivan

'All I have done I have done for Ireland
and for Ireland I am proud to die.'

After the court's sentence was carried out, the relatives of Dunne and O'Sullivan made a request to the British Home Office for leave to remove the men's remains to Ireland but their application was refused and their bodies were buried within the prison grounds.

It took many years of campaigning on the part of the National Graves Association before the British Home Office would concede to the release of the two men's bodies. On Thursday, the 6th of July 1967, two coffins holding the remains of Joseph O'Sullivan and Reginald Dunne arrived on Irish soil. They were accompanied by friends and relatives from London and a guard of honour escorted them to the pro-cathedral in Dublin. Joseph O'Sullivan's brother Patrick placed a Tricolour over the coffin of Commandant Reginald Dunne. This Tricolour was the same one which Dunne himself had placed over the coffin of Terence MacSwiney when his body was returned to Ireland in October 1920. A Tricolour was also placed over the coffin of O'Sullivan and the remains of the two men lay in state at the pro-cathedral.

In 1929, the National Graves Association unveiled a memorial to Dunne and O'Sullivan on the Republican Plot in Dean's Grange Cemetery, in the hope that the two would one day be buried there. That day came on the 8th of July 1967 when both were finally laid to rest.

At the base of this memorial is a reference to a '*Michael McInerney who died for Ireland*' Michael was a friend of the two men who died in England.

Vol. Joseph 'Sonny' Hudson - 12th August 1922

The town of Dún Laoghaire did not escape the fighting of the Civil War, which by now was engulfing the whole country. In the small village of Glasthule, to the south of the main town, an incident took place that is still the cause of debate today. Civil War, which by its very nature involves old comrades fighting one another, can and has caused deep resentment between families throughout the country which has lasted generations.

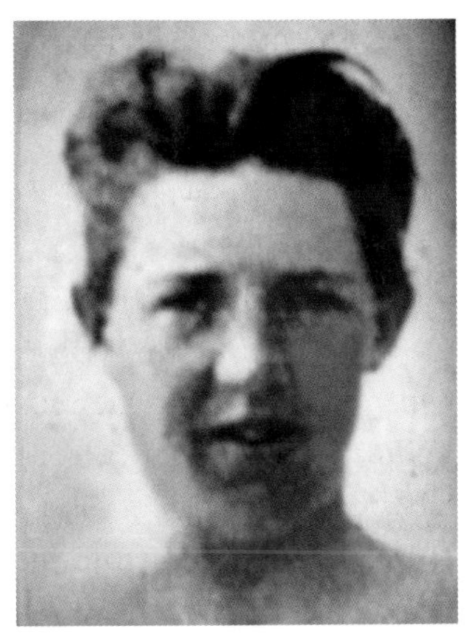

Vol. Joseph 'Sonny' Hudson

There once stood a small group of houses in Glasthule known as Carroll's Cottages, close to where the present day Congress Gardens. At these cottages, a young local man became one of the earliest victims of the war when he was shot by other local men who were now serving in the Free State Army.

On the 10th of August 1922, Joseph 'Sonny' Hudson, an IRA Volunteer, along with two other men, was examining a broken revolver in Hudson's house at 3 Carroll's Cottages. While trying to fix the gun, Sonny's younger brother ran into the kitchen and alerted them to an approaching Free State Army patrol. The three quickly ran out of the house through the back door, just as the patrol entered the street outside. The young men made a dash over the rear wall, but after realising that they had left the revolver behind on the kitchen table, Sonny returned to retrieve it. By the time he again reached the rear wall, two CID men, who were with the army patrol, entered a neighbour's house and, according to the owner who testified at the subsequent inquest, the two men in civilian clothes started firing out towards the back garden when they got to the woman's hallway. The two officers then continued out towards the yard, where both men again fired shots at the young man who was now lying wounded on the ground. On reaching the back door herself, the owner said she saw Sonny Hudson lying on a heap of stones at the rear wall and could hear him moan. She gave evidence that while Sonny was lying injured on the ground he said to the soldiers 'why did you fire when I surrendered?'

The wounded man was dragged from the back garden by National Soldiers and placed into the back of one the military lorries which they arrived in and taken to St Michael's Hospital in Dún Laoghaire.

In a statement taken from Sonny in his hospital bed just before he died, he said that:

> *'The others and myself ran out to get over the back wall. The next I heard was a shot. I heard no shout to halt before the shot was fired. Then I heard several more shots and a call to halt'*
>
> *'We did not fire a shot, as the gun was out of order. I threw the revolver into the yard. I put up my hands and shouted surrender. When my hands were up I was shot. They then pulled me through the yard into the motor and brought me to St Michael's Hospital.'*

At the inquest, the two CID men said that they were fired upon by Hudson and only returned fire in self defence. There was no evidence found at the scene that could show Hudson had fired at the men. The only bullet holes that could be found were the ones in the wall where Hudson was shot. The verdict was given, as death from

> *'a gunshot wound inflicted in the course of military operations by the Free State Army of Harbour Barracks, Dún Laoghaire'*

Mr Noyk, the solicitor acting for the military at the inquest stated that:

> *'... it was an unfortunate state of affairs, in which brother was arrayed against brother.'*

At the time of his shooting Hudson was home on leave after taken part in various operations against Free State forces in the north Wicklow area. Two months short of his 19th Birthday he died on the 12th of August 1922 and over the next year many more of his comrades would sacrifice their lives. Joseph Hudson was buried on the 16th of August in Dean's Grange Cemetery's Republican Plot. His mother and father were allowed to be buried with their son when their time came.

In 1946 a new road which had recently been constructed close to where Carroll's Cottages once stood, was named Hudson Road in honour of Sonny and the ultimate sacrifice he paid.

Ten days after his death, the leader of the Free State Forces, Michael Collins was also shot and killed during an ambush in West Cork after returning from a visit to his own family home.

Pte. Peter 'Peadar' Kenny - 20th August 1922

Forces of the National Army were fighting for and securing military barracks in many villages and towns around the country as the Civil War hostilities continued. On the other hand IRA units were once again being forced into flying columns and the use of ambush as opposed to defending garrisons which they were continually losing.

On the 20th of August 1922, a car travelling into the town of Blessington was attacked by IRA Volunteers. The car contained six members of the National Army who were heading towards the town's barracks. Blessington had only been re-captured from the IRA the previous month but small units of republicans were still very active in the area. The ambush resulted in five of the six occupants getting shot by the Volunteers, one dying instantly. The young man who died was named Peadar Kenny a private in the Free State Army. Peadar was aged 24 and lived at a house called Brooklawn on the Adelaide Road, Glasthule. His remains were removed to St Michael's Hospital in Dún Laoghaire where a post mortem was carried out. Controversy surrounded the inquest into Peadar's death as the State tried to insist that 'flat nosed bullets' were used in the ambush and that this contravened normal warfare.

On the 24th of August 1922, Pte Peadar Kenny was accorded a military funeral with full honours from Glasthule church to Dean's Grange Cemetery. A firing party consisting of soldiers from the Harbour Barracks in Dún Laoghaire fired a volley of shots overhead as his coffin was lowered into the grave. Peadar's remains were laid to rest beside those of his comrade and fellow soldier Samuel Webb, at the far end of the cemetery's West section. The Kenny family plot consists of two grave spaces bordered with limestone, and has a white marble tablet style memorial. The inscription shows that the young soldier's parents Peter Snr and Annie were also interred with him in 1950 and 1965 respectively.

John Hervey Colvill Jones - 28th August 1922

During the War of Independence, republicans found it difficult to obtain arms for their Volunteers and had to resort to raids on police stations and private houses to try and make up the shortfall. There was a more desperate need for guns during the Civil War and the IRA had to resort to tougher actions in order to acquire weapons.

On the night of the 26th of August 1922, four Volunteers approached a house called *Drangan* on the Brighton Road, Foxrock. The four men knocked on the front door and told the Jones family, who lived there, that they were looking for arms and were going to search the house. Any men who were in the house at the time were ordered into a downstairs room while the Volunteers ransacked the remaining rooms. After searching upstairs and returning to the first floor, the Volunteers were confronted by brothers Percy and John Jones. The brothers had become increasingly agitated at the raider's presence and tried in vain to get them to leave. Both men were again ordered to stand aside and to go back into the room but John, the younger of the two refused. One of the raiders raised his revolver; pointed it at John demanding that he move and when he refused was shot in the stomach.

John Jones was aged 49 and worked as a civil servant with the Land Commission. He was rushed to St Vincent's hospital where he was immediately operated on. He spent two days recovering in a nursing home but unfortunately his health deteriorated further and he died from his injuries on the 28th of August.

John's remains were removed to Dean's Grange Cemetery for burial on the 31st of August and interred in the family plot at the far end of the South section. The memorial is a large dome-shaped tablet headstone sitting on a double plot which is all constructed from limestone.

At an inquest into John's death the jury returned a verdict of 'Wilful Murder'

Vol. Charles 'Rodney' Murphy &
Vol. Edward 'Leo' Murray - 1st September 1922

Vol. Charles 'Rodney' Murphy

Not far from Dean's Grange Cemetery stands a large cottage named New Park Lodge, on the old grounds of the New Park estate which lies halfway between the villages of Dean's Grange and Stillorgan. On the night of the 31st of August 1922 four Volunteers of the IRA had arranged with an employee of the estate to be allowed to sleep at the lodge that night as they were unable to stay at home for fear of arrest.

One of the men, Charles Murphy had recently been imprisoned in Dublin's Mountjoy Jail as a member of the Anti Treaty IRA but a few days earlier was transferred to Dr Stevens Hospital for medical treatment. While in hospital he was visited by the three other men, James Nolan, Andrew O'Neill, and his cousin Edward Murray. Charles Murphy was to be returned to Mountjoy after receiving his treatment but with the help of his three friends escaped from the hospital.

Leo Murray, although only aged 19, was previously a captain in the National Army but he deserted and joined the Anti-Treaty IRA. The four men belonged to the 6th Battalion of the IRA's South Dublin Brigade and were on the run for the past few days. They knew the military authorities were looking for them as soldiers from the National Free State Army had recently raided their homes.

It was well past midnight by the time the four settled down for a good nights rest at the Lodge. The men weren't long asleep when they were awoken again by the sound of a gun shot that had come into the lodge from outside. O'Neill was slightly wounded by this shot and in a desperate attempt to escape, jumped from his bed and ran out towards the kitchen. When he reached the kitchen he heard another shot that seemed to come from the bedroom where he just left, and then a barrage of gunfire that came from outside the Lodge. By this time soldiers were attempting to get in through the front door so O'Neill ran back to the bedroom and found that Rodney Murphy and Leo Murray were both shot. Rodney received a wound to his stomach and was lying bleeding on the ground. Leo was also shot in both the head and left thigh and was still lying in his bed by the time O'Neill returned to the room.

It seems that when the men heard the first shot Murray turned to Nolan and told him that soldiers were trying to get into the lodge. Murray was in a state of panic and even considered taking his own life before allowing the soldiers get the chance, but he was hit twice by bullets and died where he was sitting up in the bed. Murphy got out of his bed and also tried to run through the doorway but was struck in the left side of the stomach and fell back into the room. O'Neill who reached the bedroom and found that his comrades were shot was quickly followed by the soldiers and captured along with Nolan.

At the inquest into the two deaths, Mrs Murray stated that soldiers in uniform from the Naval Base in Dún Laoghaire and C.I.D. officers from Oriel House (Intelligence Headquarters in Dublin) raided her home on the Wednesday before the killings and told her that they would riddle her son and make her a present of his body. The C.I.D. were plain clothes officers made up of ex-IRA Volunteers, some of whom had worked closely with Michael Collins, and former members of the Police and British Army who now were under the direction of a man named Joe McGrath.

Charles 'Rodney' Murphy was aged 22 and lived with his mother and siblings in Foxrock Close. The family home backed on to Dean's Grange Cemetery and Charles regularly used the grounds to get to and from the house without being noticed. His cousin Edward 'Leo' Murray lived at number 16 Charlemont Avenue in Dún Laoghaire town. The two men were listed in the cemetery Interment records as 'Soldiers' and were buried together in the Republican Plot. At the inquest into the killings, which was held at St Michaels Hospital Dún Laoghaire, the Coroner Dr Brennan spoke out against the troubles, saying:

> *'...it is impossible for any Irishman to express in the English language any sentence that would accurately describe the prevailing state of slaughter that existed in their country at the present day'*

The jury returned a unanimous verdict

> *'that these men met their deaths at the hands of the National Military in the discharge of their duty'.*

The bodies of both men were buried together with full military honours in what is now the Republican Plot in Dean's Grange Cemetery.

Comdt. John Joseph Stephens - 2nd September 1922

The new Free State government was desperately trying to bring the Civil War to an end and so began to adopt tougher measures in its attempts to persuade their old comrades in the Irish Republican Army from continuing the fight. The plain clothes officers from the Intelligence Headquarters in Oriel House were exceptionally ruthless and began executing IRA members who they saw as a threat or as easy targets living alone.

One such man who was seen as a threat was 33 year old Volunteer John Joe Stephens. Stephens who was originally from the town of Belleek in Co Fermanagh was recently assigned to the Dublin Brigade IRA. He was only in Dublin a few days and staying in a boarding house at number 7 Gardiner Place in the city centre.

In the early hours of the 2nd of September 1922, shouting could be heard outside the boarding house where Stephens was staying and loud knocking on the door. The owner of the large residence went to an upstairs window to ask who was at the door. A man there told the landlady to open up quickly or the front door would be burst in and so she went down stairs. When she opened the front door three men carrying revolvers walked in and asked the lady if there were men by the name of Flynn and Stephens staying in the house.

The three armed men then searched the house, finding Stephens, Flynn, and another man named Duffy in their rooms and ordered the three to get dressed and go down stairs. Stephens had asked what they wanted with him but he was only told to move quickly. He was taken down stairs along with the others and all three were asked several questions as to their political views. Stephens was not afraid and gave his views that he didn't agree with the Treaty. He was the only one they wanted and was marched from the house to a waiting car and driven away, all the time covered by the mens guns.

Later on that morning at around 6.30am a man cycling in the direction of the city to work reported to the police at Kilmainham that he saw a man wounded on the roadside about 100 meters south of Blackhorse Bridge. When the police arrived on the scene they found a man in a semi-conscious state who was bleeding heavily and who was able to give his name as John Stephens. An ambulance arrived and the injured man was then removed to Dr Steevens Hospital. Although very weak John was able to tell the police officers that he was taken from his lodgings on Gardiner Place at about four o'clock that morning by armed men who forced him into a car and drove him to where he was found. John said that the men ordered him out of the car near Blackhorse Bridge and was followed from the car by two of them. Both produced their guns and aimed them at John, shooting him in the back. Believing they had killed Stephens, the men returned to their car and drove away. Stephens said he didn't know the men and couldn't give a reason as to why they shot him. John Joe Stephens was shot a total of three times and died in hospital later that Saturday morning.

At the inquest into his death, the jury found that Stephens died from '...shock and haemorrhage, following gunshot wounds, inflicted by some person or persons unknown'.

Following his funeral, which took place on the 6th of September, the remains of Stephens were taken to Dean's Grange Cemetery and interred in the Republican Plot.

Comdt. Patrick Michael Mannion - 17th September 1922

Patrick Mannion was from County Mayo and was a Commandant in the Irish Republican Army. He was assigned to the 2nd Western Division at the start of 1922. The 22 year old was then reassigned to the Louth Brigade at the beginning of the Civil War and was known by all his friends as 'Mayo', a nickname that they admirably bestowed on him. By that September, Patrick was living at a house off the South Circular Road in Dublin and was due to take part in a planned attack on the Headquarters of the Intelligence section of the Free State forces at Oriel House in Westland Row on the 17th of September 1922.

The attack was thwarted by government forces before it ever got going, sending republican fighters fleeing from the area in all directions. While walking away from the direction of Westland Row towards the canal at the end of Mount Street, Patrick and another two republicans were called on to halt by a patrol of National Soldiers near the junction of Mount Street Bridge. The three refused to stop, and drawing their revolvers began firing at the soldiers in a frantic bid to escape. The F.S. patrol returned fire and were soon aided by a Crossley tender that was passing on its way to Beggars Bush Barracks and which also began firing in the direction of the three men. In the fighting, Mannion was wounded in the leg just below the right knee and was captured. In an act that would be considered unjustifiable in any period of warfare,

Mannion was dragged from the bridge to the corner of Clanwilliam Place. At this point a Free State officer removed his revolver and shot Patrick in the back of the head. His two comrades, who by this time had surrendered, were arrested and taken away as the body of the dead man was dumped on the side of the road.

A while later Patrick's body was removed to the nearby Sir Patrick Dun's Hospital. The following day a post mortem was carried out by the city Coroner, at the inquest which was also held at the hospital a jury established that Mannion died from '...shock and haemorrhage, caused by bullets fired, by men wearing uniform, and in our opinion, is wilful murder'. One of the jurors dissented.

Because the accusation of murder was levelled at the military and carried in a newspaper story, all subsequent articles on the matter were censored as to their content.

Patrick Mannion died on the 17th of September 1922 and following his funeral mass three days later, his remains were removed to Dean's Grange Cemetery where he was buried in a family plot. The plot is located at the edge of the pathway, just in front of the Catholic Chapel. The grave is covered over by a large tablet and is overlooked by a tall Celtic cross memorial and plinth. Patrick's inscription is etched on the left side of the plinth and reads as follows:

'Patrick M. Mannion, 2 St Catherine's Ave, S.C.R., Dublin.
Late Comb't T.O. 2nd Western Div'n,
and 'MAYO' of Louth Brigade I.R.A.
Whose life was ended at Mount St Bridge Sept 17th 1922.
Holy Mary intercede for him.'

It is believed that Mannion, Stephens, Murray, Murphy, and Hudson were all targeted for execution by the leaders of the new Free State. A murder gang was set up to hunt down certain Volunteers of the Anti-Treaty IRA; including the above named and they succeeded in killing the five men as well as many others.

Vol. Francis Michael Power - 2nd November 1922

In November 1922, the Free State government officially introduced a policy of executing republicans who were found in possession of guns or explosives. The policy was introduced chiefly by the government leaders, W.T. Cosgrave, Kevin O'Higgins and Richard Mulcahy; with O'Higgins stating that the use of terror was the only way to bring the war to an end. Under their authority a total of 77 official executions were carried out between the 17th of November 1922 and the 2nd of May 1923, which is considerably greater to that of the 14 executions officially carried out by the British government during the much longer War of Independence. It can be seen from the previous sections that many more were executed before this policy was introduced but responsibility by the government was never officially accepted.

On the day after the policy's introduction, the IRA prepared an attack on the home of Richard Mulcahy who was also the Commander-in-Chief of the Free State Army and who was seen by many as primarily responsible for introducing the execution policy. Mulcahy's residence 'Lissonfield House' was situated on the Rathmines Road near the entrance to Portobello Army Barracks and was guarded by soldiers. The gate lodge at the front of the house was used by the military as a guardroom. Volunteers involved in the operation took up positions in front of a Catholic church, which was across the road from Lissonfield House, and where a Novena mass was just ending at about 8:30 that night. Out of the darkness one of the Volunteers named Francis Power ran out on to the road and threw a bomb at the gate lodge but this failed to explode. At this point the republicans began firing on the military guard inside the lodge. The small number of guards managed to get out of the lodge through the rear window and took up a position beside the gate but by this time the firing had ceased.

While the soldiers were busy clambering through the rear window a military bike and side car travelling towards Portobello Barracks, came upon the fighting. The two officers on the bike dismounted and began firing on the Volunteers position from the flank. The Volunteers were caught off guard and immediately began to retreat, some using the crowds coming from the church to escape, while others went through a laneway further along the road. But the man who threw the bomb took the full brunt of the two officer's gun fire and was hit three times in the body. He fell in front of the church and died instantly after being hit in the head, chest, and arm. One of the officers took the gun away from the body and from a search of his clothes found a letter which was addressed to *'F.M. Power, Students Room, St Vincent's Hospital, Dublin.'*

Francis Michael Power was aged 22 and was from Hogan's Pass, Nenagh in Co Tipperary. He was living in Dublin at the time of his death and studying as a medical student at St Vincent's hospital.

After his death, the Free State authorities refused to release Francis's remains to his family for requiem mass and burial. On the night before he was buried, members of the IRA's Dublin Brigade broke into the morgue where his body was held and removed it. His remains were buried in a family plot in the cemetery at Dean's Grange on the 5th of November 1922. The headstone consists of three marble plinths and cross. At some point the cross was damaged and it now lies on the ground in front of the plinths. Power's grave is situated directly behind the Kavanagh vault at the top of the main walkway.

Cpl. Samuel M. Webb & Harry G. Manning - 13th November 1922

Ulverton Road is a section of the main thoroughfare between the towns of Dún Laoghaire and Dalkey and lies between Castle Park School and Castle Street Dalkey. During the day time this road would have carried trams but would have been dark and secluded place by night.

On the 13th of November 1922 a patrol of National soldiers of the Free State Army were returning to Dalkey barracks with a prisoner along Ulverton Road. At about 11 o'clock that night, as the foot patrol made its way along the dark and winding road, they came under attack from an IRA unit positioned behind rocks in a nearby field. A bomb was thrown at the soldiers and the Volunteers then began to open fire with rifles, revolvers and a Thompson gun. The National soldiers were vulnerable in open ground that afforded little cover and three of them were shot within seconds. Other members of the patrol managed to return fire, but another bomb was thrown before the IRA unit made their escape.

One of the National soldiers named Samuel Webb was shot a number of times and died on the road from his injuries. Webb was 20 years old and lived locally in Glasthule. The other two soldiers were not badly injured and later removed to Monkstown Hospital.

Unfortunately, a civilian who happened to be passing along Ulverton Road at the time of the attack, was also shot. Harry Manning, aged 43, was returning towards his home at Bullock Harbour after visiting his brother-in-law in Killiney and was only a few hundred yards from his home when the attack occurred. Harry received a shot through the ear and died instantly alone with Corporal Webb.

On the 16th of November 1922, the remains of both men were conveyed to Dean's Grange for burial. Harry Manning was laid to rest in the South section just behind the offices; there is no marker on his grave today.

Samuel Webb who received full military honours at his funeral was laid to rest in the West. His grave is at the far end of the section and only a few graves in off the second last pathway. The grave has a limestone cross with floral design which sits on top of four plinths. There is also a small cast iron railing which surrounds the plot. The inscription which is barely legible, states as follows:

In Loving Memory
of my dear son Samuel Webb
Who was killed 13 Nov 1922 aged 20 years
R.I.P.
Sweet heart of Jesus have mercy on his soul
Erected by his loving mother

The Irish Civil War was officially brought to an end in late May 1923, with the total number of deaths nationwide believed to be in the region of 3000. Although the 'Free State' eventually brought the war to a close, random executions of republicans; both inside and outside the prisons continued well past May 1923. The appalling actions which the newly formed government took against IRA Volunteers during the Civil War left deep scars both physically and mentally on the people of Ireland and in particular those republicans that survived.

Not far from Dean's Grange lies the quiet seaside village of Booterstown.It was here on the 10th of July 1927, while on his way to Sunday Mass that Kevin O'Higgins, Vice President, and Minister for Justice was approached by three Volunteers of the IRA and shot dead. O'Higgins was one of the most controversial figures of the war and would become one of the last participants to be killed as a result.

Notable People

'And what shall we do for timber?
The last of the woods is down.
Kilcash and the house of its glory,
and the bell of the house are gone.
The spot where that lady waited,
who shamed all women for grace,
when earls came sailing to greet her
and mass was said in the place.'

From the poem 'Kilcash' by Frank O'Connor

Dean's Grange Cemetery would not be the first place that springs to mind when someone thinks of the burial places of Ireland's famous citizens. The cemetery does not hold the graves of historical giants like Collins, de Valera, Parnell, and O'Connell who are all interred in Glasnevin, but buried here are quite a few remarkable figures who have shaped the Ireland of today in different ways.

I use the term 'notable' when I write about these people as I want not only to acknowledge some of those; who in their own right are famous, but those who have contributed to life by lesser known acts or by simply the reasons which led to their death.

There are those who equally deserve to be acknowledged in this publication but I won't have included them all. I would certainly love to write about every person interred in the cemetery that is famous in their own specific fields, but I have not, either because I have not come across them or because they were included in other publications like 'Dean's Grange Cemetery' by Vicky Cremin, 'Dublin Burial Grounds & Graveyards' by Vivien Igoe and other such publications.

Those I have chosen to cover will be admired and hated by different readers. They will be considered by some to be idols, patriotic or unpatriotic or even controversial and by others to be irrelevant. But they all have an importance to someone or for some thing and for that reason I have decided to write about each of them.

Personally, I have enjoyed discovering each of these people and their life stories. I have included where possible a summary of their life, careers, and the reasons they have been included. I have also attempted to give an air of expression to each of them through something they said or which was said of them. At the end of each piece I have listed where in the cemetery they are buried and their plot number. This number along with everyone else mentioned in the book can be found in The List of Graves at the rear of the book.

Kathleen Behan - Mother of All the Behans

Kathleen Behan, to me sums up the type of person who is not well known but someone who I consider has contributed greatly to life and to the lives of those around her.

Kathleen was a typical mother of her era, raising a family during some of the harshest times in recent history, with poverty, death, war, and epidemics constantly hanging above the heads of every family in Ireland.

Born in 1889, Kathleen Kearney lived with her parents in Dublin city until she was nine years of age. It was then that the young girl was sent off to an orphanage after her father died and her mother could no longer take care of her. She left the orphanage at the age of 15 and moved back in with her mother in the south inner city.

Kathleen married her first husband Jack Furlong in 1916, the same year he would be imprisoned for his part in the 1916 Rising. A year later further tragedy hit the young family when Jack died of a 'flu epidemic leaving her a widow of two young children. Kathleen managed to find a relatively good job as a clerk with Dublin Corporation. In 1922 Kathleen married again, this time to a man by the name of Stephen Behan. Stephen was another republican and was involved in the fighting during the Civil War. He was arrested in 1922 and he was imprisoned for the second time, again the family would suffer. A few months after Kathleen gave birth to their first son Brendan and later they had another four children.

They were a family of literary brilliance with Brendan becoming a poet, novelist and playwright and dedicated republican, he was imprisoned a number of times for activities with the Irish Republican Army. Another son, Brian, also became a fine novelist and wrote the autobiographical book 'Mother of all the Behans' about Kathleen. Dominic became a novelist and Playwright and also wrote short stories and songs, most notably 'Come Out Ye Black & Tans'. The ability to write which was shown by her sons can be traced back to Kathleen's older brother Peader Kearney who famously penned the words of the Irish national anthem, 'Amhrán na bhFiann' in 1907.

She had a hard life like many, raising a young family in the tenements of Dublin, which at the time were considered worse than the slums of Calcutta. The family moved out of the tenements in the 1930s to Kildare Road, Crumlin, but times would continue to be tough. Her son Brendan was imprisoned for the first time, in a Borstal in England and then later in Irish jails.

Her husband of 45 years; Stephen died in 1967. Kathleen went on to become a well liked folk singer, recording the song 'When All The World Was Young' in 1981 and frequently appeared on television.

On the 26th of April 1984 Kathleen Behan died in her Raheny nursing home at the age of 95. Her coffin was draped in the tri-colour as the cortege made its way into the cemetery. Mattie O'Neill, a family friend spoke at the grave side saying:

> *'Kathleen had lived a full and fruitful life and has gone tranquilly and joyfully in her 95th year to where she believed age and infirmity do not exist and all sorrow ceases'*

She is buried in the St Anne's section, which is to the top left hand side of the grounds. There is no headstone on her grave bar some flowers and blowing in the wind a small tri-colour. But this woman has left behind a legacy and you could say that her family are an appropriate memorial.

Louie Bennett - Irish Women Workers Union

There are many women buried in Dean's Grange Cemetery that have contributed to Irish and international society in many ways, but Louie Bennett is a little different. Louie spent the best part of her life working endlessly for civil and human rights, causes she held dear to her heart.

She was born on the 7th of January 1870 into a moderately wealthy family; her father was an auctioneer in Dublin city and they lived at the family home in Blackrock not far from Dean's Grange village. In her teens she attended Alexandra College in Dublin, later going to London and then to Bonn, Germany where she studied music. During her life Louie wrote a number of novels, amongst them: 'The Proving of Pricilla (1902)' and 'A Prisoner of his World: A Tale of Real Happenings (1908)'.

On returning to Dublin she became involved in the Irish suffrage movement and in 1911 co-founded the Irish Woman's Suffrage Federation. She was tirelessly involved in activities against the 1913 Lockouts, helping those affected most by the strike. She was a pacifist who opposed the Easter Rising of 1916 and both World Wars. But it was the rights of women that particularly motivated Louie, who became General Secretary of the Irish Woman's Workers Union in 1917; a position she held until she retired in 1955. She acted as a mediator during the Civil War and later helped to form the Irish Association to foster better relations between Northern and Southern Ireland. She actively sought world peace and represented Ireland on the Woman's International League for Peace and Freedom. She was elected to the executive of the Labour Party in 1927, standing unsuccessfully for the party in the General Election of 1944. In 1932 Louie became the first woman president of the Irish Trade Union Congress. She fought successfully for changes to the new Irish Constitution of 1937 focusing on women's equality or the lack of it for that matter. In a letter to her close friend Hanna Sheehy Skeffington, Louie remarked:

'I suppose when the necessity of knitting socks is over,
the order will be 'bear sons!' And those of us who can't will
feel we had better get out of the way as quickly as we can.'

Louie was relating to a belief at the time that if women weren't knitting socks for soldiers then they should be giving birth to them. She never married or raised a family of her own.

In 1956, the year after she retired from the IWWU, Louie Bennett died at her home in 'St Brigids' Killiney on the 25th of November, she was aged 86. Her remains were interred with those of her parents and brother, in a double plot located in the South-West section, between the Glorney vault and Protestant chapel. The memorial consists of a large granite domed shaped headstone which has a marble face on which '*Louisa Bessie*' and the words '*Lead kindly light*' are inscribed.

Richard Irvine Best - Celtic Scholar

Richard Irvine Best was born in Derry in 1872. He was educated at the Foyle College in the city and later went on to study Gaelic under Henri d'Arbois de Jubinville in Paris. While in Paris he translated the latter's book *Le Cycle mythologique Irlandais* into English and became a renowned Celtic scholar, which was incidentally listed in the cemetery records as his profession. He was awarded the prestigious Royal Prussian Academy's 'Leibniz Medal' in 1914 and was congratulated by Albert Einstein. He also received honorary degrees from TCD and NUI.

He associated with the likes of James Joyce and John Millington Synge. Joyce even included him in his book 'Ulysses', in the chapter Scylla and Charybdis where it seems he was mockingly portrayed during the scene discussing Shakespeare, which took place in the National Library. Another friend George Moore also included him in his own book, *Hail and Farewell.*

'Best is John's (Eglinton) coadjutor in the National Library: a young man with beautiful shining hair and features so fine and delicate that many a young girl must have dreamed of him at her casement window, and would have loved him if he had not been so passionately interested in the in-fixed pronoun-one of the great difficulties of ancient Irish.'

Richard wrote a number of books himself, primarily his dual-volume publication 'Bibliography of Irish Philology' and 'Manuscript Literature' 1913-1941.

In 1903, Best along with John Strachan and Kuno Meyer, had set up the School of Irish Learning in Dublin. He was Director of the National Library of Ireland from 1924–40, Senior Professor of Celtic Studies at the Dublin Institute of Advanced Studies 1940–47, President of the Royal Irish Academy 1943-46 and he also became Chairman of the Irish Manuscripts Commission 1948-56.

He died in his residence at 57 Upper Lesson Street Dublin on the 25th of September 1959 aged 88 years. His grave is located in the South-West section between the Glorney vault and the Protestant chapel. The grave is marked with a large dome-shaped marble headstone which sits on a granite plinth and kerbing. The inscription as well as listing Best's achievements, also states that his wife 'Edith Oldham' was buried nine years before him and that she was an

'Associate & Hon. Associate of the Royal College of Music London.' His friend, Thomas Lyster, who was Chief Librarian at the National Library of Ireland, and who was himself included by Joyce in the same chapter of 'Ulysses', is also buried in the Cemetery. The Lyster family's double grave is situated on the pathway to the right of the offices and is marked by a large rectangular granite headstone.

James Byrne - Martyr of the 1913 Lockout

On Saturday, the 1st of November 2003, a monument was unveiled in Dean's Grange Cemetery to mark the grave of James Byrne, martyr of the infamous 1913 Lockout. The unveiling of this monument was the result of work carried out by four trade union members, Jason McLean, Seamus Fitzpatrick, Brian Riddick, and this writer, who all believed that Byrne at the very least deserved a memorial upon his grave.

The remains of James Byrne's original headstone

James was born in the town of Dún Laoghaire and it was here that he would later marry his fiancée Nora. The couple moved into their new house at 5 Clarence Street and were blessed with eight children. Byrne was an ardent trade unionist and follower of socialists like Jim Larkin and James Connolly. His belief in the right of the worker led him to become secretary of Dún Laoghaire branch of the Irish Transport & General Workers Union and secretary of the Dún Laoghaire and Bray Trades Councils. In this capacity Byrne led his fellow Tramway workers out on strike in opposition to William Murphy and other prominent Dublin employer's refusal to recognise Trade Unions.

Described as a man of big stature, Byrne was arrested in Dún Laoghaire on the 20th of October 1913 and charged with 'assault and intimidation' of an employee who passed the pickets of 'Messrs Heiton & Co, Coal Merchants'.

He was locked up in a cold and damp cell in Mountjoy Prison while awaiting trial on the charges, and in protest to the conditions and the refusal to grant him bail; he undertook a hunger and thirst strike. After only a few days the authorities gave in and released Byrne on bail until his trial could be heard. But the damp prison conditions and hunger strike had taken their toll on the 'Big' man. Byrne fell ill with pneumonia and was soon removed from his home in Dún Laoghaire to the nearby Monkstown Hospital. It was here on the 1st of November 1913 that the 35 year old lost his fight for life. James Byrne left behind a widow and six children, two of their young children passed away in the years before his death.

It was reported in the Irish Times that on the morning of James Byrne's funeral, as many as three thousand people attended the procession as it made its way to Dean's Grange Cemetery. The funeral left Byrne's home and took two hours to travel through the streets towards his final destination. Outside the cemetery grounds, James Connolly climbed on top of a cab and during an impassioned speech said of James Byrne...

'My heart swells with pride that the workers are at long last learning to honour their fighters and martyrs. James Byrne died a martyr as any other man who died for Ireland'

One fight had just ended but the fight for the rights of the working classes continued and Irish workers would eventually win their rights and trade union membership.

Those who knew of Byrne's burial place believed that no headstone was ever erected on the grave and that James Byrne was a forgotten hero. On Easter Saturday 2002, local republicans were erecting a cross on Byrne's grave and while searching for stones to place around the cross two young boys found a small piece of marble bearing half an inscription. Another piece was soon discovered in the undergrowth nearby and the two pieces turned out to be what was left of James Byrne's original headstone. The discovery of the headstone and full inscription had shown that this man was not forgotten, least of all by his wife. The marble stone was erected by Nora Byrne in memory of her husband and their two young girls. It measured no more than 18 inches in length and was incorporated into the final monument that was unveiled the following year. The grave of James Byrne lies in the cemetery's West section, and it is surrounded by a small group of trees. It is situated to the right of the Republican Plot. The new monument stands as a testament to his sacrifice and for future generations to pay homage.

Joseph Campbell – Poet / Nationalist

Joseph Campbell was born into a nationalist family in Belfast on the 15th of July 1879. His father ran his own construction company, which in turn allowed his young son to receive a good education. He studied both the English and Irish languages and later attended St Malachy's College in Belfast.

Campbell travelled to Dublin in 1902 where he became involved in nationalist literary circles and began contributing articles to papers such as the *United Irishman.* Along with his friend Herbert Hughes, he compiled *Songs of Uladh* (Songs of Ulster) in 1904, with both men writing the song 'My Lagan Love'. His repertoire of books of poetry includes T*he Garden of the Bees* 1905, *The Grilly of Christ* 1907, *The Mountainy Singer* 1909, *Irishry* 1913, *Earth of Cualann* 1917, some of which he penned under his Gaelic name 'Seosamh Mac Cathmhaoil'.

'I am the mountainy singer, the voice of the peasants dream.
The cry of the wind on the wooded hill, the leap of the fish in the stream.'

He also wrote plays such as *The Little Cowherd of Slainge* and *Judgement*, a two part play that was performed in the Abbey Theatre in 1912.

Campbell founded the Ulster Literary Theatre in 1904 and on moving to London the following year began working with Irish literary societies, while also keeping up work as an English teacher. It was while he was in London that he met Nancy Maude and the couple later married in May 1910. They moved back to Ireland in 1911 and settled in Co Wicklow.

In 1913 Campbell became active within the Irish Volunteers as a recruiting officer and publicist. During the 1916 Rising he helped as a medical orderly and later became a Sinn Féin Councillor in Co Wicklow. The *Collected works of Pádraic H. Pearse* was transcribed into English by Campbell in 1917. He sided with other Anti-Treaty republicans during the Civil War and was imprisoned for 18 months. His captivity caused his profound hatred of the new Irish politics and when he separated from Nancy in 1925; Campbell emigrated to the United States.

While in America he quickly set about founding the School of Irish Studies in New York that same year. He became a lecturer at New York's Fordham University from 1927 to 1938 during which time he also founded the Irish Foundation in 1931 and re-established and edited the 'Irish Review' newspaper in 1934.

Campbell returned to Ireland in 1939 and settled at Lackandaragh near Glencullen Co Wicklow. He loved the 'Garden of Ireland' and many of his writings include stories which are surrounded by its landscape. It was here in his small isolated cottage that he died on the 6th of June 1944; aged 65. Later that year, the writer Austin Clarke wrote about his death:

'In the spring of 1944 his nearest neighbours in the glen noticed that no turf smoke was coming from the chimney and became alarmed. The poet was found dead where he had fallen across the hearthstone.'

Joseph is buried in a plot alongside his sister Josephine and her husband Samuel Waddell. Samuel was also a writer / stage actor who used the pseudonym 'Rutherford Mayne'. The double plot is situated directly up from the turnstile gate and is on the left hand side of the pathway. The headstone consists of a small granite cross with plinths and bears the three names, under Joseph's name is inscribed the word 'poet'.

Anastasia Carey – 1st Interment in Dean's Grange Cemetery

The first burial to take place in Dean's Grange Cemetery was of a woman named Anastasia Carey. The interment took place on the 28th of January 1865. Anastasia was working as a 'servant' for the nuns of the St Josephs Orphanage on Tivoli Road, Dún Laoghaire, when an epidemic of typhus fever broke out. She contracted the illness and after a short time succumbed to its deadly effect. She died on the 27th of January 1865 and, because of the urgency of the epidemic, her remains were interred the following day. The grave of the 41 year old is located at the top of the lower North section, on the opposite side of the pathway from the Catholic chapel. It is the plot of the St Josephs Orphanage and consists of three graves which are surrounded by railings. Her own headstone is inscribed with the following words:

'Pray for the repose of the soul of Anastasia Carey,
who died of Typhus Fever caught in the discharge of her duty

at St Josephs Orphanage during the prevalence of an epidemic 27th January 1865. Aged 40 years.'

A number of years after I had written down the above inscription the three memorials in the plot were refaced with polished granite. The old engraving, which was hand cut and in italic script was more refined and in fitting with that era, as opposed to the new polished granite which I feel takes away from the whole memorial and its significance within the cemetery.

Kathleen Clarke - Revolutionary Woman / Caitlín Bean Uí Chléirigh - Mrs Thomas Clarke

Born Kathleen Daly in Limerick on the 11th of April 1878, she became the wife of Thomas Clarke the leader of the 1916 Rising who along with her brother Edward Daly were executed for their active roles that week. Kathleen came from a very republican family in Limerick; her uncle John Daly was a well known Fenian who became Lord Mayor of the city in 1899. She met her husband Thomas Clarke through her uncle, in the summer of 1899. The couple married in New York in July 1901, later having three sons.

They returned to Ireland in November 1907 in order for Thomas to organise the Irish Republican Brotherhood and Kathleen herself became a founding member of Cumann na mBan in 1914. After the Rising, Kathleen was arrested along with many other republicans and held in Dublin Castle. On the evening of the 2nd of May 1916 Kathleen was taken from her cell to meet with her husband for the last time in Kilmainham Jail. The following morning Thomas was executed in the prison yard.

After his death, Kathleen became involved with the Irish Volunteers Dependants Fund. She was again arrested in June 1918 and imprisoned in Holloway Jail, England for the charade 'German Plot' and was released the following February.

She was very active during the War of Independence and was elected unopposed to the second Dáil as a Sinn Féin TD for mid Dublin in May 1921. She stood with the Anti-Treaty side and lost her seat in the June 1922 General Election and only regained it in the short lived 1927 election, when the Dáil only lasted from June to September. Kathleen stood again during the general election in 1948, this time for Clann na Poblachta but was unsuccessful. She was previously elected to the Seanad Éireann in 1928 and held this position for two terms.

In 1939, she joined the Fianna Fáil Executive and became a member of Dublin Corporation. She was elected as Lord Mayor of Dublin in June 1939, the first woman to have ever held this position. She was Lord Mayor until 1941 and left the Fianna Fáil party that same year citing the corruption of other party members for her decision to leave. She spent the rest of her life close to her family and was never far from the political scene, attending many functions and giving speeches.

Kathleen Clarke died in a Liverpool nursing home on the 29th of September 1972. Her remains were conveyed to Dublin where she received the honour of a State funeral to Dean's Grange Cemetery. On the way from the Pro Cathedral the funeral cortege paused outside the G.P.O. for one minute as a further mark of respect. Her remains were laid to rest beside those of her eldest son John Daly Clarke, just off the main drive in St Brigid's. The headstone is of polished granite and has the following inscription in Gaelic text:

'I ndil chuimhne ar Chaitlin Ui Chleirigh
(baintreach Tomáis S. Uí Cléirigh a básaíodh
I mBaile Átha Cliath bealtaine 3 1916)
A d'éag meán fómhair 29 1972 in aois 94 bliana.
A chroí ró-naofa iosa, dean trócaire ar a hanam.'

The inscription loosely translates to: 'In memory of Kathleen Clarke (widow Thomas J. Clarke died in Dublin 3rd May 1916) Died September 29th 1972 aged 94 years. Sacred heart of Jesus, have mercy on her soul.'

In a quote from her book *My Fight for Ireland's Freedom*, Kathleen said that on the morning of the 1916 Rising she turned to her husband Thomas and said . . .

'I often told you that if it came to a parting of this kind,
I would become a poltroon. Am I one now when I ask you
if there is any way out with honour other that what you
are doing, going to certain death, with all hope of success gone?
I feel I want to take you and hide you away, save you at all cost.'

Mary Edith Coleman – Red Cross Nurse / Iron Cross Recipient

Behind the cemetery office, just a few steps along the pathway nearest the wall, you will notice a tall pedestal memorial carved out of marble to your right. The memorial marks the burial plot of Mary Edith Coleman. Mary lived at a house suitably named 'Marylodge' Williamstown near Dean's Grange with her husband Charles Coleman, who she met after her first marriage. Marylodge became what is known today as the Blackrock Clinic.

Mary served with the Red Cross Society during the Franco-Prussian War 1870-1871 and was mainly stationed close to the front near Saarbrücken on the French German border. When the war ended, Emperor William of Prussia awarded her the prestigious Iron Cross in recognition for her care of injured soldiers from both sides of the fighting. This award was obviously something that she and her family were very proud of as it forms the main element of her headstone's inscription . . .

'For her devoted care of the wounded soldiers both French and
German in the Franco-Prussian War in the year 1870 under
the auspices of the Red Cross Society, she was Mrs Alsager, decorated
by the Emperor William with the Order of the Iron Cross.'

My attempts to research further into Mary's background came to a dead end each time. There can't be too many people in Ireland least of all a nurse, who has received this award and for so little to be known about her.

Mary Coleman died at Blackrock on the 23rd of September 1906 at the age of 67.

Sybil Connolly - Clothes Designer

Born Sybil Veronica Connolly in Swansea, Wales on the 24th of January 1921, she moved to Waterford in 1936 after the death of her Irish born father. At the age of 17, Sybil returned to the UK again; this time to London in order to take up a fashion apprenticeship with 'Bradley & Co'. It was here that she would gain the experience in the finer details of dress making that would ultimately lead to her success as a future cloths designer.

Due to the Second World War and its effect on London, Sybil returned to Ireland in 1940 where she took up a position with the Dublin clothing firm 'Richard Alan'. By the mid 1950s her traditional designs with her use of Irish fabrics were attracting interest, chiefly from the American market. In 1957 Sybil left Richard Alan and opened her own fashion house 'Sybil Connolly Inc' at 71 Merrion Square Dublin. Included amongst the most famous of her clients were, Elizabeth Taylor, Jackie Kennedy, and Julie Andrews and this is just to name a few.

It was during the 1950s and 60s that Sybil really became an international name for design and placed Ireland on the map of world fashion. She was a traditionalist who liked her clothes to be of an old fashioned design that were not only elegant but that the customer was comfortable wearing. Sybil was an old fashioned lady and as trends changed in the sixties she refused to change with them, stating that...

'I never liked the mini and I always remember what Dior once said to me in Paris' 'A woman should show her curves not her joints'

Sybil did not go along with the changes in fashion but broadened her design ideas to include a wide range of ceramics and crystal ware for Tiffany & Co New York and also wrote a number of books on gardening and interior design.

Sybil Connolly died on the 6th of May 1998 at the age of 77, and was buried in Dean's Grange Cemetery. It was requested on the morning of her funeral that if anyone outside of her family were to ask where she was to be buried that the location should not be given. I believe that this was at Miss Connolly's own personal request, and as it was asked then it should be the same now.

John A Costello – Fine Gael Politician / An Taoiseach

John Aloysius Costello was born in Dublin on the 20th of June 1891. He was educated in the city by the O'Connell Irish Christian Brothers School and later at third level in UCD. He went on to study Law at the Kings Inn, becoming a Barrister in 1914. In 1922 he became an assistant to the Attorney General and in 1926 became the Attorney General under the Cumann na nGaedhael government and would also represent Ireland at the League of Nations.

He was removed from the office as Attorney General in 1932 when Fianna Fáil took power but the following year was elected for the first time as a TD (Teachta Dála) for Dublin County, becoming a member of the newly established Fine Gael party. The new Fine Gael party was made up of elements of Cumann na nGaedhael, the National Centre Party, and the Army Comrades Association otherwise known as the 'Blueshirts' in opposition to Fianna Fáil. The government had outlawed the Blueshirts organisation and was in the process of introducing a Bill to ban the wearing of uniforms in public. John Costello opposed the Bill and during its debate in the Dáil in February 1934, said:

> *'The Minister gave extracts from various laws on the continent, but he carefully refrained from drawing attention to the fact that the Blackshirts were victorious in Italy and that the Hitler Shirts were victorious in Germany, as, assuredly, in spite of this bill and in spite of the Public Safety Act, the Blue Shirts will be victorious in the Irish Free State…'*

Fine Gael didn't gain power for another 14 years and when they finally did, it was only possible through an inter-party coalition. Costello was asked to become Taoiseach of this Fine Gael led government from 1948–51, since the then leader of Fine Gael Richard Mulcahy was considered an unacceptable choice as Taoiseach because of his controversial role during the Civil War.

Under Costello's leadership, the Irish Government in 1948 declared Ireland a 'Republic' after the repeal of the External Relations Act with Britain. Costello stated . . .

'There was no reason why Éire should not continue in association with Britain but not as a formal member of the British Commonwealth . . . the External Relations Act was full of inaccuracies and infirmities and the only thing to do was to scrap it.'

The party lost power in 1951 when Costello called an election, having been in government for only two years, but they were returned to power again in 1954. He became Taoiseach once again until 1957, when the government was brought down, in part as a result of the IRA border campaign. It was after this that Costello re-dedicated himself to his work as a barrister and settled as a backbench TD until he retired from mainstream politics in 1969. In recognition of his political work, John Costello was made a Freeman of Dublin City in 1975. He died in Dublin early the following year on the 5th of January aged 84.

On the 7th of January 1976, the remains of John A. Costello were conveyed to Dean's Grange Cemetery. His family had requested a simple funeral and declined the State funeral usually afforded all Taoisigh on their death. His remains were interred with those of his wife Ida, who had passed away 20 years earlier. The grave is situated just off the third pathway along St Patrick's. The memorial has a unique architectural design of a marble tablet face with inscription and which rests against an elongated limestone cross.

John Boyd Dunlop – Inventor of the first functional pneumatic tyre

John Boyd Dunlop was born on a farm in Ayrshire Scotland on the 5th of February 1840. He was educated locally and went on and studied to become a Vet at an Edinburgh Veterinary College, a profession he practised for a number of years before moving to Belfast in 1867. During his time in Belfast, Dunlop found that the cobbled streets were difficult for the solid tyres of bicycles, making travelling around very difficult. In 1887, he took the wheel of his son's bicycle and wrapped thin layers of rubber around its outer rim and then gluing them together he created an air tight tube in which he was able to inflate with air. His idea worked and the following year Dunlop patented his invention. By 1889 he put the manufacture of his tyre into production, opening up a factory in Dublin. Two years later he extended his plant to Birmingham England.

But Dunlop was to discover that another Scottish man had first patented the idea in 1846 and his patent was deemed invalid. However Dunlop was able to continue his production and soon almost every new tyre in use; had the Dunlop name.

In 1890 he went into partnership with a man named Du Cros and both men worked hard developing the company over the next six years. For some reason in 1896 Dunlop sold his interest in the company and also the patent for £2,000 and Dunlop retired to Dublin, never making any real profit from his idea. The Dunlop Rubber Company went on to become a very successful business and is still manufacturing what we know today as Dunlop Tyres.

John Boyd Dunlop died in Dublin aged 81 on the 23rd of October 1921. His remains were interred in a grave to the left hand side of the Glorney vault in the cemetery's South-West section. He is buried along with his wife Margaret and some of his children. The memorial consists of a marble mantelpiece with his name, place of birth and dates. Part of the headstone inscription reads as follows:

'Behold the upright for the end of that man is peace.'

James (Jimmy) Dunne – Irish and English Football Legend

James (Jimmy) Dunne

Jimmy Dunne was born on the 3rd of September 1905 in Ringsend Dublin. The young man who mostly played centre forward in a number of Dublin minor teams began his senior career at the age of 18 when he was signed by Shamrock Rovers. He spent much of his time at the club with the reserves and after two years decided to accept a starting position with English Third Division (north) team New Brighton in 1925.

Dunne got off to a great start at New Brighton, scoring six goals in eight games, with his goal scoring abilities quickly grabbing the attention of the bigger clubs in England. In February 1926 he was signed by First Division, Sheffield United who placed him as an apprentice with the reserves. It wasn't until the 1929-30 season that Dunne started playing as a regular with the first team. He scored his first hat-trick in September 1929 against Portsmouth and more surprisingly all three were from headers. Dunne ended the season as the Leagues highest goal scorer with another hat-trick and double four goal hauls.

In the 1930-31 season he scored a total of 41 goals, which still stands as the most scored by an Irishman in one English league season, and 50 goals if you count the Cup. He would knock in over 30 goals in each of the First Division seasons between 1930 and 1933. Looking back over his time with the Sheffield United from 1926 to 1933, Dunne managed to score 143 goals in 173 games, which is an amazing feat for any professional player today.

Again Dunne's talents were being watched by other clubs and in 1932 Sheffield United turned down an offer of £10,000 for the Irishman. However he moved to Arsenal the following year at a reduced fee after Sheffield ran into financial difficulties. His first year with the club was good with Dunne scoring a total of nine goals, helping Arsenal to win the 1933-34 First Division title. But things would turn against the player when Arsenal signed the future England International Ted Drake in 1934 resulting in Dunne losing his first team place. The newspapers remarked that Dunne was 'the most expensive reserve player in English football' a swipe directed at the Arsenal management.

Dunne ended his English career in the Second Division playing with Southampton where he scored 14 goals in 36 appearances for the club, becoming their highest scorer. He remained with Southampton for the 1936-37 seasons and returned to Shamrock Rovers as player-manager in 1937.

Under his stewardship Rovers won the League of Ireland in 1938 and 1939 and in 1940 took the FAI Cup title. He went on to manage Bohemians, between the years 1942-47 before returning again to take charge of Shamrock Rovers.

Apart from his club football Dunne had an illustrious career in Irish International teams during the late 20's and throughout the 1930's. He played in both F.A.I. (Southern) and I.F.A. (Northern) Ireland teams as both sides claimed to represent the whole country. He played a total of 15 games with the F.A.I. scoring 13 goals in all. When the Ireland team travelled to Europe in 1939, they passed through the port of Southampton on their way. On walking down the gangway Jimmy Dunne was greeted with applause from the Dockers in tribute to his time at the local club.

On the 14th of November 1949, Jimmy Dunne died suddenly of a heart attack at his home on Tritonville Road, Dublin. He was 44 years old and was still managing Shamrock Rovers. His funeral travelled to Dean's Grange Cemetery where his remains were buried in St Ita's section. His grave is located at the far end of the section close to the wall and is marked by a marble Tablet headstone in the form of a Celtic cross. His family had placed a ceramic picture of the footballer on the headstone but it has since faded with time.

Just inside the turnstile gate lie the remains of another great Irish Footballer named Peter Farrell. Peter played alongside Jimmy Dunne when they were both with Shamrock Rovers. Farrell later went on to play 11 seasons with Everton and was captain for 7. He was part of the 1949 Ireland squad which beat England 2-0 in Everton's home ground of Goodison Park, Ireland becoming the first team outside of the UK to beat England at home and Peter becoming one of the goal scorers.

Barry Fitzgerald - see William Shields

Donal Foley - Journalist / Author

Donal Foley was born on the 4th of September 1922 in Ring, a Gaeltacht area of Co Waterford, where his family spent their summer holidays. The family lived in the small village of Ferrybank, situated on the north side of the River Suir in Waterford city where his father was the local national school teacher. Foley attended the National School in Ferrybank and was heavily influenced by his father's teaching and politics and was a fluent Irish speaker. He later studied in the city's St Patrick's College of which he had many happy memories playing hurling and courting girls. Hurling was not just a sport, it was a passion passed down from his father, and which he cherished his whole life.

Donal Foley left Waterford for London in September 1944, a strange destination as London was still in the grip of war. But like many, there was no work to be found in Ireland and shortly after arriving found work for a time on the railways. In 1950 Foley began working for the Irish Press in London after persistently submitting articles to the paper's Fleet Street office. He began writing daily columns for the paper, beginning with his first article 'In Britain Today'. It was while working in Fleet Street he befriended Irish writers like Brendan Behan and Patrick Kavanagh. Foley later wrote about his experiences living in England, focusing on Irish communities, the social scene of pubs, the loss of the Irish language by new immigrants and on the British press's mocking view on Ireland and her people. In 1955 Donal became a journalist with the London office of the *Irish Time*s and in 1963 moved back to Ireland to become the paper's news editor.

Donal brought many changes to the paper. He wrote in and edited the Irish language current affairs column 'Tuarascail' and actively encouraged women journalists to make more active contributions to the pages. In 1977 Foley was appointed Deputy Editor. Without any doubt, Foley will be best remembered for his own satirical column 'Man Bites Dog' which appeared weekly in the paper and was also reprinted into an annual publication for ten years running. The following is taking from part of the column which he wrote in December 1970, under the heading 'Innocence T.D.'

'Mr Charles Haughey's horse, is a favourite choice as a Fianna Fail candidate for the next by-election whenever it occurs. The party feels that it is now strong enough to nominate a horse.
A Fianna Fail party spokesman said 'it is time we had some sound horse sense in the Dail. We will however, draw a line at political horse trading.' In Leinster House last night it was pointed out that the electors, had, in the past been saddled with much worse candidates.'

In 1977 Foley wrote and published his own autobiography *Three Villages*. In the book he relates his life from growing up in Waterford and his time spent in England, to his return back to a new Ireland right until shortly before his death. Foley lived with his wife in Mount Merrion and died in hospital at the age of 57 on the 7th of July 1981. His remains were interred in the centre of St Anne's section where his grave today has no headstone. There is a plaque at the head of the grave which contains the following inscription:

'Brendan Foley died 19th December 1975 aged 17 years.
Donal Foley died 7th July 1981 aged 57 years.
Ar dheis Dé go raibh a n-anamacha uaisle'

The Gaelic inscription below reads as: 'May their noble souls be on God's right side'.

Sir Howard Grubb - Telescope Designer

If you are involved in astronomy or you have a specific interest in Telescopes, then the name Howard Grubb is notable and stands as a byword of excellence. When he was alive, Grubb was the best known designer and manufacture of telescopes in the world.

Howard Grubb followed in his father's footsteps and began working with the family business 'Grubb Telescope Company' in 1865. His designs excelled the company's reputation to that of the finest manufactures in the world and the demand for Howard's telescopes soared. The company supplied telescopes and additional equipment to observatories around the world such as Melbourne in 1869, Vienna in 1881 and to others like Madrid and Mississippi. Grubb telescopes are still in use today and can be found at Observatories at University College Cork, Dunsink in Dublin and at Armagh.

The Grubb's were also manufacturers of periscopes and gun sights and undertook all work at their offices in Rathmines. The company had to relocate to England during the First World War, since the threat from German submarines in the Irish Sea was considered too dangerous. At the time they were supplying most of their equipment to the Allied forces.

Over the years his designs improved, with the noted advantage of making the controls smaller and moving them closer to the eye piece. This allowed the astronomer to move the scope without having to take their eye off the lens. After the war Howard went into partnership with Charles Parsons, the inventor of the steam turbine and the company was renamed Grubb-Parsons. This new company was at the forefront of telescope design for many years to come. The last telescope manufactured by Grubb-Parsons was at La Palma on the Canary Islands in 1984, still one of the most important of its kind in the world and a fitting memorial to the Grubb family.

It is safe to say that Howard's designs had, without doubt, advanced the work of astronomy throughout the world. In 1883 he was elected a fellow of the Royal Society, and in 1887 was knighted by the Lord Lieutenant of Ireland for his remarkable skill. On his 82nd birthday, Howard received a testimonial from the UK's leading astronomers stating:

> *'We recall with admiration his devoted application of his resourcefulness and ingenuity to the development of the instrumental equipment of astronomers through more than sixty years . . . his contribution to the undertaking of the Photographic Survey of the heavens, in the provision of suitable object glasses, and of the refined clockwork needed for the accurate movement of the telescopes.'*

Howard Grubb died at his residence in Monkstown on the 16th of September 1931; he was aged 88. His remains were interred in the South-West section, with those of his wife Mary, who died only five months earlier. The double grave is located in the centre of the section, close to the West and is marked by a marble cross with plinths.

Augustine Henry - Botanist / Physician

Augustine Henry was born in Dundee Scotland on the 2nd of July 1857and while still a young boy moved with his parents to Cookstown Co Tyrone. He was educated at the Cookstown Academy and went on to study Natural Science and Philosophy in Galway. He later received a Masters Degree in Arts from Queens University Belfast before finally receiving a Medical Degree in 1879.

After a time studying the Mandarin Chinese language, he went on to work as a Physician with the Chinese Imperial Maritime Customs

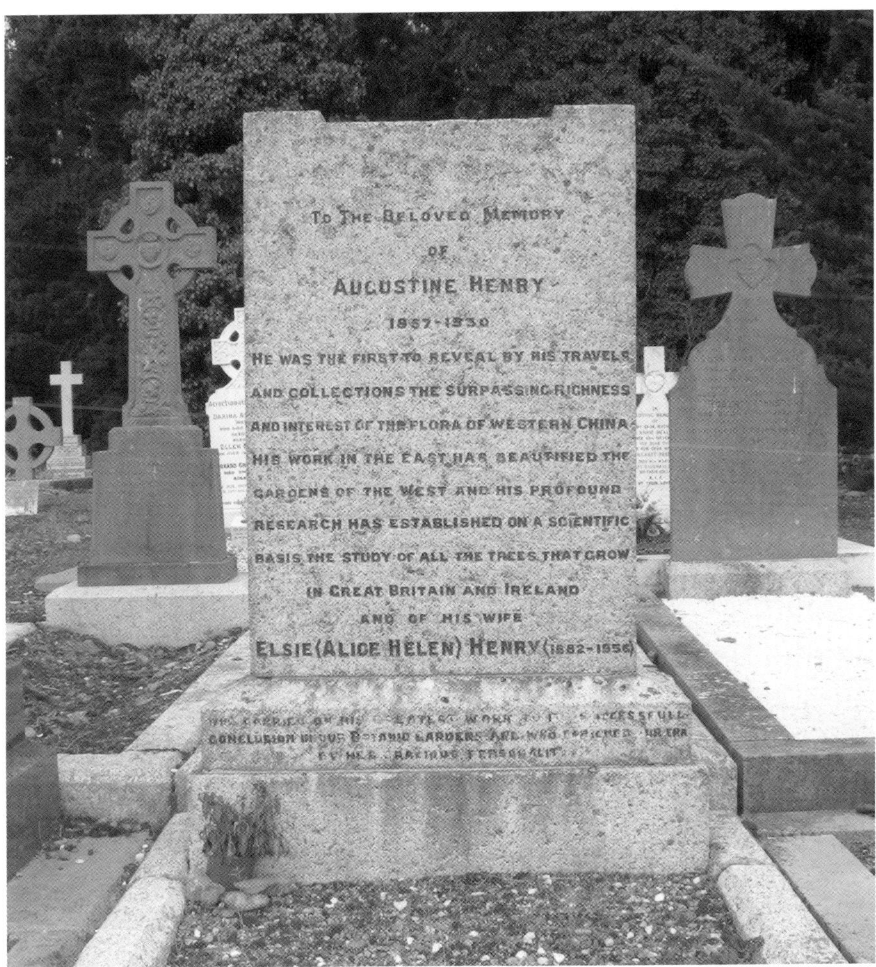

Augustine Henry headstone

Service in 1881, spending a total of 20 years with the service and travelling throughout Asia. His work brought him into contact with many of the native Asian plants and this in turn led him in the search of ingredients for new medicine. Henry's meticulous cataloguing of Asian plants began. By 1889 he sent the first of many specimens to Kew Gardens in London. Over the next ten years he sent thousands more dried and live plant specimens including seeds to Kew and the Botanic Gardens in Dublin. Many of these have become well known garden plants and some species even include his name: *Carolinella henryi, Clematis henryi, Rhododendron augustinii, Lilium henryi* and *Viborium henryi.*

He published a list of Chinese plants with their informal names in the journal of the Royal Asiatic Society in 1888. He also came in contact with a secluded race known as Lolo in south-west China in 1888. Henry recorded a dictionary of their language which up until that point was unknown. Later he moved to Taiwan and it was while there that he began studying Taiwanese Law.

Henry left China in 1900 and went on to study Forestry in France. He developed the School of Forestry in Oxford in 1905 and was Reader in Forestry at Cambridge in 1908. That same year he married Alice Brunton. He returned to Ireland in 1913 after he was offered the position of Professor in Forestry at the College of Science in Dublin (UCD). His work would eventually lead to the founding of the Irish National Forestry Service. He and his friend Henry Elwes wrote the *The Trees of Britain and Ireland*, 1907–13. He was interested in the Celtic Revival and was a friend of W. B. Yeats. After his death in 1930, his wife Alice completed the logging of his private collection of over 10,000 species, that now form the Augustine Henry Forestry Herbarium in Glasnevin's Botanic Gardens.

Augustine Henry died at the age of 73 while in his home at Sandford Terrace in Ranelagh on the 23rd of March 1930. His remains were buried just off the main walkway, between the Glorney vault and the Consecration Cross, in the upper part of the North Section. His rectangular pink-granite headstone reads:

'To the beloved memory of Augustine Henry 1857 – 1930.
He was the first to reveal by his travels and collections,
the surpassing richness and interest of the flora of Western China.
His work in the East has beautified the gardens of the West
and his profound research has established on a scientific basis,
the study of all the trees that grow in Great Britain and Ireland.

And of his wife Elsie (Alice Helen) Henry (1882-1956), who carried on his greatest work to its successful conclusion in our Botanic Gardens and who enriched our era by her gracious personality.'

Noel Thomas Jenkinson – Trade Unionist / Republican / Communist

Noel Jenkinson was born in Loughcrew, Co Meath in 1929. When his father was offered a job as a gardener in Dún Laoghaire the family moved to the area and eventually settled in Sallynoggin. Like many Irishmen Jenkinson emigrated to England, finding work as Bus Conductor in London. He worked hard at his job and became secretary of the local branch of the T&GWU trade union. He also joined the Communist Party and became very active in the campaign for civil rights in the North of Ireland. But things were to change drastically for Noel when on the 22nd of February 1972 the 'Official IRA' bombed Aldershot barracks, the home of the British Army's Parachute regiment. The Official IRA stated that they carried out the bombing in retaliation of the Regiment's shooting dead of 14 unarmed civilians in Derry the previous month, which became known as 'Bloody Sunday'.

Three men were subsequently arrested and charged with the bombing; one of them was Noel Jenkinson. Two of the men were subsequently acquitted, the third Jenkinson, was convicted virtually on the basis of his political beliefs as no forensic evidence was produced. The trial Judge Sebag Shaw took part in the cross-examination and questioned him on his support for communism. The police planted fake evidence at Jenkinson's flat in a bid to place him in Aldershot on the day but during the trial this evidence, a shop receipt, turned out to belong to the son of a Chief Inspector who was also one of the investigating officers. But at the end of the trial Jenkinson was still convicted and he became the first person in England to be given a recommended sentence, receiving 30 years imprisonment.

An appeal was lodged with the European Court of Human Rights in Strasburg but this was rejected, Noel always maintained he was innocent. Noel was violently attacked on three different occasions while he was incarcerated and on the 9th of October 1976 was found dead in his cell in Leicester Prison, he was aged 46. Although he died under mysterious circumstances an inquest found that he died as a result of heart attack.

His body was flown back to Ireland and was brought to Dean's Grange Cemetery and laid to rest in St Mogue's section. His last place of residence was listed in the cemetery records as 'Leicester England'. There is a small headstone marking the grave and at the bottom of his memorial inscription is 'Venceremos' which is a recognised republican motto which translates into 'Victory'. Noel's name is listed on the Republican Roll of Honour for those who died during the troubles.

Peter Judge - Actor F. J. McCormick /
Eileen Judge – Actress (nee Crowe)

Peter Judge was born in Skerries North Dublin in 1890. Eileen Crowe was born in 1899 and along with Peter were renowned members of the Abbey Theatre. The couple married in 1925 and began raising a young family, with their careers continuing to centre on the Abbey Theatre and their different film roles. Judge acted under the stage name of F. J. McCormick, because during his early career he was employed as a civil servant and was unable to use his real name.

Judge joined the Abbey Theatre in 1918 and Crowe later becoming an Abbey actress in 1921. At the time she joined, the playwright Lennox Robinson best described her when he said:

> *'From the first audition she gave me, I knew we had an actress and a voice and then suddenly she knew she was an actress, pulled up her socks and worked like a demon at her profession.'*

The couple married in 1925 and combined their family lives with the Abbey. They both took acting roles in Seán O'Casey's play *The Plough*

Part of the memorial on the grave of Peter Judge (actor F. J. McCormick) and Eileen Judge, actress (nee Crowe)

and the Stars (1926) which was set around the Dublin tenements during the 1916 Rising. Judge played the part of 'Capt Brennan' of the Irish Citizen Army whilst Crowe that of 'Bessie Burgess' the fearless and sometimes foul mouthed lady of the tenements. They continued in these positions when the play was turned into a film in 1936.

Judge acted in a total of three films while Crowe had parts in twelve, most of them after Peter's death. Judge acted in and directed Ireland's first drama film *Fun at a Finglas Fair* (1916). The film was destroyed during the 1916 Rising when British soldiers ransacked the Masterpiece Picture House, where the film was shown. His most notable part was in the film *Odd Man Out* (1947) when he played 'Shell' an amusing small time criminal in post WWII Belfast. He appeared along with Eileen in the film *Hungry Hill* (1947). Judge didn't like the Hollywood type filming and after *Odd Man Out* would concentrate mainly with theatre, his main professional love, and interest. He died in Dublin on the 24th of April 1947, just before the release of *Hungry Hill.* Ernest Blythe director of the Abbey Theatre said, on learning of Peter's death:

'In his death this country has lost one of the most notable men of our generation and the world has lost one of the greatest artists of our time.'

Eileen carried on with her acting career appearing in a further nine films, amongst them *The Quiet Man* (1952) and *Shake Hands with the Devil* (1959). She played the starring roll in *Boyd's Shop* (1960) and a short documentary *Cradle of Genius* (1961), which was nominated for an Oscar the following year.

Eileen died at home on the 8th of May 1978 and was buried with her husband in St Patrick's section. There is a very interesting memorial on the couple's grave which was designed by the celebrated Cork sculptor Seamus Murphy. The memorial measures roughly eight feet high and is made of limestone. At the top of the stone, Murphy has carved out the theatre faces 'happy and sad\, a fitting tribute to one of the greatest couples of Irish stage and film.

Seán Lemass - Fianna Fáil Politician / An Taoiseach

John Francis Lemass was born in Ballybrack Dublin on the 15th of July 1899. At the age of 15 he joined the Irish Volunteers and during the 1916 Easter Rising was stationed in the GPO, the Volunteers headquarters on O'Connell Street. Seán was arrested after the Rising but due to his young age was released and allowed to continue his education with the Christian Brothers. He remained active within the IRA to such a point that he was involved in the infamous execution of British agents in November 1920, which became known as the first Bloody Sunday. Lemass was arrested again the following December and released 12 months later after the signing of the Anglo-Irish Treaty. He chose to take the Anti-Treaty side and during the Civil War was arrested and imprisoned again until June 1923.

Seán married his wife Kathleen in August 1924 and by that November was elected to Dáil Eireann for the first time as a Sinn Féin TD (Teachta Dála) in the constituency of Dublin South. In 1926 Sinn Féin refused to let its members sign the Oath of Allegiance in order to enter the Dáil, and so Lemass and others resigned and formed a new political party. He proposed that the new party be called The Republican Party but Éamon de Valera insisted on Fianna Fáil, as a compromise the party's full title includes both names.

Fianna Fáil won power in 1932 and Lemass was appointed Minister for Industry and Commerce. Unlike many then in Fianna Fáil this position suited a conservative politician like Lemass and the future decisions that would have to be made. Under his ministerial leadership, the Industrial Credit Corporation was established which facilitated the setting up of semi-State bodies like, Bord na Móna, Aer Lingus and Irish Sugar Limited (Siúcra). He proved to be very skilful at his ministerial position and held it on four separate occasions between 1932 and 1959. He was made Minister for Supplies during WWII and by the end of the war in 1945 Lemass was chosen to be Tánaiste (deputy Taoiseach) and held this position on three separate occasions between 1945 and 1959. Poverty and unemployment in Ireland were rife since the foundation of the State and in October 1955 Lemass presented his idea for economic change to the Fianna Fáil party. This change, he said could not be secured solely by the State and proposed that private investment was the way forward.

> *'The aims of the proposals are, firstly, to give the national economy the necessary initial boost; secondly, to bring about an increase in private investment activity to the extent required to secure an adequate and continuing expansion of the scope and efficiency of private productive enterprise; and thirdly, to show that the effort needed is not beyond the country's possibilities.'*

His idea soon became the policy of Fianna Fáil and they won the 1957 general election. Lemass's popularity grew within the party and he eventually succeeded Éamon de Valera as leader and became Taoiseach in 1959.

During his tenure in 1965, Lemass became the first Irish leader to visit the Northern State at Stormont. He decided to retire as Fianna Fáil

Taoiseach and did so in the Dáil in November 1966. He settled easily into the backbenches before finally retiring as a TD in 1969. He displayed in his work the true characteristics of the man he was and would probably be regarded as the finest Taoiseach that Ireland ever had.

Sean Lemass died in hospital on the 11th of May 1971 at the age of 71. He was afforded a State funeral to his final resting place in Dean's Grange Cemetery. Lemass was buried in a grave at the edge of the main drive in St Patrick's. Today the grave also holds the remains of his wife Kathleen and it is marked by a very simple limestone Celtic cross with a marble face.

Philip Francis Little - First Minister of Newfoundland

Philip Francis Little was born to Irish parents on Prince Edward Island in 1824. He was educated in Charlottetown and studied Law before eventually becoming a Solicitor and finally qualifying as a Barrister in 1844. Philip moved to St John's Newfoundland the following year to continue his legal work and after successfully appealing an act that gave preference to local solicitors he was able to set up business in 1848.

At that time, Newfoundland was run by a representative assembly but direct rule was overseen by an appointed Governor and committee directed by London. Little became involved in politics and joined the Liberal Party which actively sought responsible government for the colony. In 1850 he stood in a by-election at the age of 26, campaigning for reform and the rights of Catholics, and won the seat by a small majority. By 1852 Philip was leading the Liberal reform party, tirelessly campaigning for responsible government for Newfoundland. He petitioned the British government on a number of occasions demanding direct rule and finally achieved this in 1855. The Liberal party won a majority of seats in the new House of Assembly and Little became the first Prime Minister of Newfoundland; all by the age of 31.

He decided to retire as First Minister after only three years in office and was appointed a judge to the Supreme Court. He travelled to

Philip Francis Little

Ireland in 1864 where he met and married 19 year old Mary Jane Holdright from Dún Laoghaire. They had a total of ten children - eight boys and two girls. He remained on as a Judge in Newfoundland until 1868 when he moved with his family back to Ireland. They settled in Monkstown near Dean's Grange, where Little looked after his in-laws holdings and his own newly acquired properties. He also worked as a lawyer in Dublin and participated politically in the struggle for Home Rule. When Isaac Butt died in 1879, Little replaced him as president of the Home Rule League. Philip Francis Little spent the rest of his days in Ireland, residing at his home in Brighton Terrace in Monkstown and it was here, on the 21st of October 1897, that he died at the age of 74. His remains were interred in a grave to the side of the walkway which runs along side the Catholic chapel. His headstone consists of a large Celtic cross with the following inscription at the base:

Sacred to the memory of
the Honourable Philip Francis Little,
The first Premier of the colony of Newfoundland,
and late a Judge of the Supreme Court,
Newfoundland,
Died October 21st 1897, aged 74. R.I.P.
'In te Domine, speravi, non confundar in aeternum'
And of his wife
Mary Jane,
who died on the 29th of March 1914, aged 69.
R.I.P.

The Latin quote within the inscription translates into: 'In thee, O lord, have I hoped, let me never be confounded.'

Donagh MacDonagh - District Justice / Poet / Playwright

Born in Dublin on the 22nd of November 1912, Donagh MacDonagh was orphaned at a very young age. His father, Thomas MacDonagh, was executed as one of the leaders of the 1916 Rising and as a signatory to the Proclamation. The following year his mother Muriel died in a swimming accident. Donagh spent a long time as a child in hospital due to ill health but this never held him back in any way. He was educated at Belvedere College, Dublin and later studied Law at UCD. He became a barrister in 1935 and was chosen as a district justice for Wexford in 1941. He was first married to Maura Smyth and after she died in 1939 married again, this time to his first wife's sister, Nuala Smyth. He had 4 children between the two marriages.

Throughout 1940-1950 Donagh presented Radio Éireann's 'Ireland is Singing' which was very popular during the war years. He was described as a poet, dramatist, and writer and will be best remembered for his play, *Happy as Larry* (1946). Some more plays included *Gods Gentry* (1951) about Irish Travellers and *Step in the Hollow* (1957).

He had a passion for Gaelic traditions and co-edited *The Oxford Book of Irish Verse* along with Lennox Robinson in 1958. He wrote the poem 'Dublin Made Me' where MacDonagh talks of the contrasts of Dublin and rural Ireland:

'Dublin made me and no little town,
with the country closing in on its streets.
The cattle walking proudly on its pavements,
the jobbers, the gombeenmen and the cheats.'

His collections of poems were published in two separate volumes 'The Hungry Grass (1947)' and 'A Warning to Conquerors (1968)' which was published after his death.

He died, aged 55, while serving as a District Justice on the 1st of January 1968. His grave can be found when you enter the cemetery through the turnstile gate and walk about 150 meters directly ahead. The grave is three spaces into the right; off the pathway. These three rows of graves to the right hand side of the pathway stretch from the gate up as far as the top of St Patrick's, and are within the North section. The point where these graves back on to St Patrick's is where the old boundary wall would have once stood before the latter section was constructed. The small MacDonagh headstone and surrounds are made of granite and are inscribed with the following short inscriptions:

'Maura MacDonagh
18th Feb 1939
Donagh MacDonagh
1st Jan 1968
Naula MacDonagh
14th Oct 1970'

William Maher - Hero of the *Leinster* Disaster

William Maher worked as a stoker aboard the RMS *Leinster* and was on the ship when she was attacked and sunk by a German U-boat on the 10th of October 1918. William was among the few people that survived the sinking and like the others he had to take his chances by entering the cold waters as the ship quickly sank. A strong swimmer, William managed get himself to an upturned lifeboat and climb on to the side. He served with the Royal Irish Fusiliers during the Boer War and would have been in some tricky situations before. There were others clinging for dear life to the raft and, in particular, a young girl named Dorothy Toppin. William held onto this 13 year old girl for two-and-a-half hours before a rescue launch arrived. As he was helping the girl's mother on to the launch, Dorothy slipped from the side of the raft into the water beneath. Without any hesitation William dove straight into the water and was able to rescue the girl and get her safely back to the launch. For his part in saving the lives

William Maher

of a total of three people, William was awarded a silver medal and certificate for bravery from the Royal Humane Society in 1919. At the same time, the young girl, Dorothy Toppin, presented him with a watch in appreciation for saving her life that day. The following inscription was engraved on the back of the watch:

'To William Maher, from Dorothy Toppin.
As a small token of gratitude for saving her life.
Leinster Disaster 10th October 1918.'

William was a very strong athletic-looking man, with a large wide moustache that added to the character of the now 'local hero'. Men in Dún Laoghaire still recall when they were young boys and how they all looked up to William and how each wanted to be a hero just like him.

William Maher died on the 11th of June 1953. He was aged 78 and had spent the last remaining years of his life with only one leg, after suffering a serious accident. At the time of his death, William still lived in Dún Laoghaire at 52 Desmond Avenue, along with his wife Elizabeth. The local hero's remains were buried in Dean's Grange Cemetery but, sadly, to this day no headstone marks the spot where he and his wife Elizabeth are buried. The unmarked grave is situated in the centre of the St Nessans section.

John Count McCormack - Tenor

John Francis McCormack was born on the 14th of June 1884 in Athlone Co Westmeath. He was educated locally by the Marist Brothers and later received a scholarship to Sligo's Summerhill College. He graduated from the college in 1902 and began singing with the Palestrina Choir at Dublin's Pro-Cathedral. He was entered by friends into the 1903 Feis Ceoil (Music Festival) in Dublin, at which he won the Tenor's Gold Medal after singing 'The Snowy Breasted Pearl' causing the audience to stand and roar in applause. By the following year, McCormack was singing at the St Louis World Fair in the US and began to make recordings with the Edison & Bell Company. In 1905, he travelled to Milan and received training from the renowned maestro, Vincenzo Sabatini, making his operatic debut in January 1906. On the 2nd of July, he married his fiancée Lily Foley; they would eventually have two children, a boy, and girl.

He was singing in operas at Convent Garden in London by 1907, becoming the youngest tenor to appear in 'Cavalleria Rusticana'. In 1909, McCormack was back in the US, singing mainly opera in New York. He was concerned about what critics were writing about his operatic acting and in 1912 began to concentrate more on his own concert performances. He toured between London, New York, and Australia, even throughout the First World War. In 1918, he was involved with fundraising for the families of those lost in the sinking of RMS *Leinster* just outside the port of Dún Laoghaire. His brother-in-law, Thomas Foley (brother of McCormack's wife Lilly), perished on the RMS *Leinster* along with his wife Charlotte. As a result of their deaths left ten children were left orphaned. The McCormacks adopted the youngest child Kevin, and made provision for the rearing and education of the other nine.

McCormack loved performing in the United States and in 1919 became a US citizen. In Monte Carlo, on St Patrick's Day 1923, McCormack appeared in his last opera. His first film role came in 1929 with *Song o' My Heart* and then in 1937, he performed in *Wings of the Morning*. Amongst the honours that he received throughout his career, was that of a 'Freeman of Dublin City' bestowed in 1923. Pope Pius XI awarded him the title of 'Papal Count' in 1928, and from that point onward he included the title in his name, henceforth being known as 'John Count McCormack'.

McCormack is best remembered for singing 'Panis Angelicus' during the Eucharistic Congress in 1932, when he sang to an estimated one million people in the Phoenix Park, Dublin.

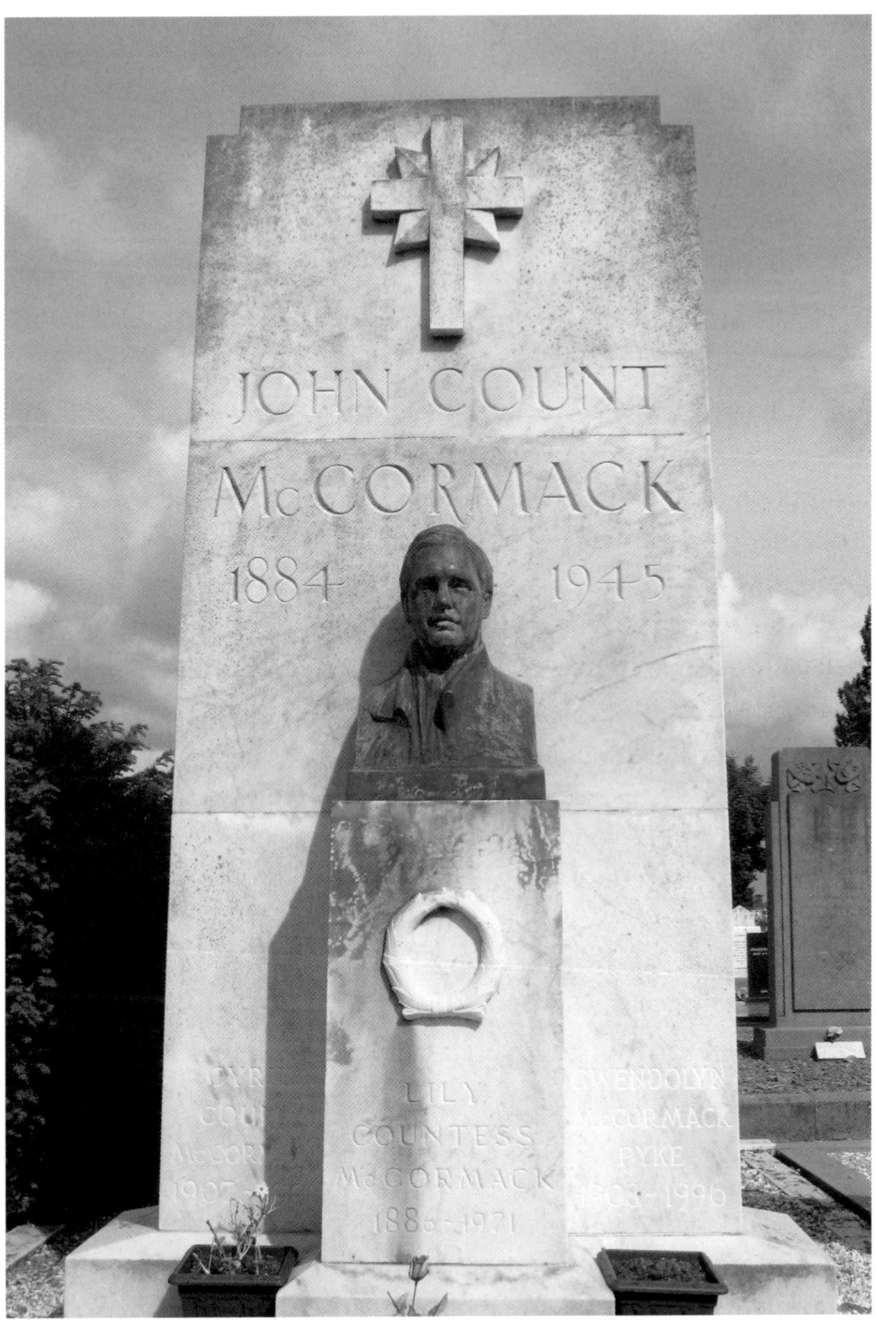

The memorial of John 'Count' McCormack

Although he announced his retirement in the U.S. in 1937 he continued to perform, but nothing on the scale of his previous years. During the harsh years of World War II he undertook concerts in order to raise money for the Red Cross. He last performed in 1942 before becoming ill with a throat infection and by 1943 recorded the last of his singing.

McCormack loved Irish ballads and one of his greatest hits, 'It's a long way to Tipperary', became a popular marching song with soldiers during WWI. His lyrics are still popular today and can be found in most music outlets throughout the country.

John McCormack died at his residence *Glena,* not far from the cemetery on the Rock Road, Booterstown, on the 16th of September 1945. He was aged 61. On the morning of his burial in Dean's Grange Cemetery, the Palestrina Choir of the Pro-Cathedral sang the 'Benedictus'. At his grave today stands a large rectangular marble headstone that measures about 12 feet in height. On a pedestal to the front of this memorial sits a beautifully crafted bronze bust of McCormack, sculpted by Seamus Murphy. The plot consisting of four graves is situated in the middle of St Patrick's section, along the third pathway.

'I dream at night of operas and concerts in which I have had
my share of success. Now like the old Irish minstrel,
I have hung up my harp because my songs are all sung.'

In 1996 the grave in which John McCormack was buried, had to be opened when his daughter Gwendolyn died and was to be interred with him. When a grave is dug for the first time, the gravedigger tries to reduce the amount of clay he has to dig out by keeping the 'hole' as it is called, to the shape and size of the coffin. Afterwards, the grave will always keep this shape as the clay that is back filled into the grave never compacts as hard. This grave kept its shape, and looking into the opening you would be forgiven for thinking that the man must have been a giant!

Joseph McGrath - Politician / Founder of Irish Sweepstakes

Joe McGrath was born in Dublin in 1887. He worked as a paper seller when he was a young boy and later joined a Dublin accountancy firm. He also had an interest in nationalist politics and became a member of the Irish Volunteers. Joseph took part in the 1916 Rising and afterwards was arrested and imprisoned in England. He stood as a Sinn Féin candidate in the 1918 General Election, which he won and represented St James's Division of Dublin city in the first Dáil and was appointed Minister for Labour. He was elected again as a Sinn Féin TD in 1921-22 and after the Anglo-Irish Treaty, supported it in the third Dáil 1922-23.

From 1922-24, McGrath held the posts of Minister for Labour and then Industry & Commerce. It was during the fourth Dáil, which sat from 1923-27, that he became a member of the newly formed Cumann na nGaedhael party but resigned his post as Minister in April 1924 over a dispute involving officers of the Irish Army. Because of the end of the Civil War, the government wanted to demobilise many of the army officers. He was unhappy with the decision since, like himself, most of the officers had previously served with the IRA. McGrath eventually resigned from the Dáil, stating:

'Government by a clique and by officialdom of old regime'

He was making the point that the new power was in no way better than the old British one.

In 1930 McGrath set up the Irish Hospitals Trust (Sweepstakes) with R. J. Duggan a bookmaker. The idea was to help raise funds for Irish hospitals, but in the process it made the two men very wealthy. Within a few years it was the largest lottery in the world, taking much of its profit from England and the United States, where gambling was still illegal.

With his new found wealth, McGrath ventured into horse racing and breeding. His most famous horse 'Arctic Prince' won the Epsom Derby in 1951. He was a member of various equestrian boards including the Turf Club, Irish Racing Board, and the Bloodstock Breeding Association of which he was President in 1953.

Joe McGrath died at his home, Cabinteely House (on the grounds of what is now Cabinteely Park), on the 26th of March 1966; at the age of 73. His burial monument bears all the trimmings of his wealth, with the entire McGrath plot consisting of six graves featuring a large, ornate marble monument that depicts the dying Christ in the arms of his mother, Mary. This plot is situated to the top left-hand corner of St Patrick's.

Dermot Morgan - Fr Ted / Actor Comedian

On the 28th of February 1998, one of Irelands best loved comedians Dermot Morgan died suddenly at his home in England. Morgan was born in Dublin on the 3rd of March 1952 and was educated at Oatlands College, Stillorgan and later at third level in nearby UCD, where he studied English and Philosophy. After graduating from college, Morgan took up teaching, but gave this up in 1976, after only two years, to concentrate full time on his career as an actor.

He began acting alongside Mike Murphy on the RTE show 'Live Mike', in which pranks were directed against members of the public and other unsuspecting celebrities. He appeared in a comedy section of the 'Kenny Live' show in the late 1980s, but this was cut for a more publicly acceptable sketch. In 1985, Dermot released a single titled 'Thank you very much, Mr Eastwood'. The song was a skit on the boxer Barry McGuigan and, like most of Morgan's humour, involved, amongst others, the clergy and the Pope.

Morgan had a great talent for mimicry and in the satirical radio show 'Scrap Saturday', he singled out many political and religious figures for ridicule. Its most popular act was that made-up to be between the then Taoiseach Charles Haughey and his advisor P. J. Mara.

Under public outcry, 'Scrap Saturday' was axed by RTE in 1991, with Morgan describing RTE's decision to end the show as being politically influenced, especially at a time when it was one of the most popular shows on Irish radio.

Dermot Morgan's big break came in 1995, when he was cast as Father Ted Crilly in Channel 4's sitcom 'Father Ted'. The show, which ran for three seasons from April 1995 until May 1998, achieved cult status through its satirical depiction of the Catholic Church. The hair-brained antics in the parochial house of Fathers Ted, Dougal, and Jack along with their barmy house keeper, Mrs Doyle, have and will undoubtedly continue to keep viewers entertained for years to come. In his most famous and most used line from the show Ted would emphatically try and explain the reason why money from a charity event ended up in his personal bank account,

'I swear, that money was just resting in my account'

The show won critical acclaim and, in 1996, was awarded three BAFTA awards, with Morgan receiving one personally for best actor.

Dermot had just finished filming the third series of Father Ted and had announced that he intended to retire from the show. While hosting a dinner party at his home to celebrate the final shoot of Farther Ted, Dermot became ill and sadly died of a heart attack. He was in the prime of his career and was only three days away from his 46th birthday. His remains were later cremated and it is believed that they were scattered over the grave containing the remains of his parents and young sister. This grave is located in St Patrick's section, and is to the right hand side just off the pathway leading to John Count McCormack's plot, in from the main drive. His family have placed a small granite plaque on the grave which reads:

'Dermot Morgan 1952 - 1998.
Brilliant, Loving, & Loved'

Delia Murphy – Ballad Singer

Delia Murphy was born in Claremorris, Co Mayo on the 16th of January 1902. She came from a wealthy family, her father making his fortune from gold prospecting in America. Delia loved singing from an early age; learning many of her first songs around traveller camp fires near her family home. She was educated in Tuam, Co Galway and in Dublin and finally went on to study at University College Galway, where she met Thomas Kiernan, whom she married in 1924.

Thomas joined the Irish Diplomatic Services and the couple soon moved to England. They returned to Ireland in 1935 and Delia started recording with the music company HMV, many of her songs becoming popular Radio requests. She appeared in the film *Men of Ireland* (1938), which was set in the Blasket Islands. In 1941 she moved to Rome, where Thomas was appointed the Irish Ambassador. While there during WWII, she was part of a network that helped many Jewish families and others, avoid capture by the Nazis. Delia would always travel to where Thomas's work as Irish Ambassador took him: Australia 1946, Germany 1955, Canada 1957, and finally, America 1960. Her talent as an Irish ballad singer thrilled audiences where ever she went and during the early 1950s she toured Ireland singing in concerts. By the end of her career Delia had amassed a recording collection of nearly 400 songs; the most popular were 'The Spinning Wheel' and 'If I Were a Blackbird'. Delia's strong Mayo accent added substance to her songs and gave the listener a real sense of Irish music.

Her husband, Thomas, died in 1969 and Delia moved back to Dublin. Fifteen months after his death, Delia Murphy herself died suddenly on the 12th of February 1971 at the age of 69 years.

The renowned ballad singer Liam Clancy said of Delia after her death: 'I think her main contribution was that she made us feel that we could respectably sing our own songs...' He was referring to the fact that he believed Delia was responsible for the revival of the singing of Irish ballads, which up until the 1930s, was in decline.

Delia's grave is located at the far end of St Brigid's section, two graves in from the main drive. There is a medium sized dome shaped granite headstone marking the plot.

(Sir) John Gardiner Nutting - 1st Baronet of St Helens

In the centre of the South-West section, directly opposite the Protestant chapel, it would be difficult not to notice a monument, which is by far the cemetery's largest and one that is most unique. This monument covers a vault in which lie the remains of Sir John Gardiner Nutting. John Nutting was the 1st Baron of St Helens Stillorgan, which is now the St Helen's SAS Radisson Hotel.

Nutting was born on the 24th of July 1852. He was educated at Clifton College Bristol and went on to further education in Germany. His appreciations of education would lead him to fund scholarships in Dublin's Trinity College in 1906 and was Governor of the Free Oxmanstown School which he also funded. He had an amazing appetite for work which included Justice of the Peace for the county of Dublin and Deputy-Lieutentant for the county and city and in 1895 was made High Sheriff. He was a Unionist politician and stood unsuccessfully in the 1906 General Election for West Hampstead.

As well as his public duties, Nutting held a large portfolio of commercial interests. He was the governor of the Rotunda Hospital and director of the Royal City of Dublin Hospital. As Chairman of the Dublin & Kingstown Railway Company, he helped fund the amalgamation of the Great Southern and Western, and Limerick and Waterford railways. This was at a time when the prospect of war was looming, the railway companies were financially cautious, Nutting purchased shares worth £250.000, no small amount of money at that time, and the works commenced.

He was Chairman and largest shareholder of E. & J. Bourke, who were the main bottlers of Arthur Guinness & Son. He held shares in wine and insurance companies and one of his other business interests was in property. In 1899, Nutting purchased St Helen's House in Stillorgan and with his vast wealth, set about refurbishing the house, and included ornate designs within its new architecture.

The creativity with which Nutting renovated St Helen's can also be found in his burial monument. There are clear similarities between St Helens and the monument in Dean's Grange which has steps leading to an area surrounded by a balustrade. The head of the platform embodies the entrance to St Helens and on which the inscription is etched. On this platform there are three large stone tablets which cover the entrance to the vault. The monument has a granite base with the remainder made entirely of limestone. It covers an area the size of ten burial plots, and also holds the remains of his eldest daughter Hilda who died in 1887at the age of 12.

John Nutting passed away at home in St Helens on the 18th of February 1918 after a long illness and was survived by his wife Mary and five children.

Frank O'Connor – Author and Short Story Writer

Born on the 17th of September 1903 to Michael O'Donovan and Mary O'Connor of Douglas Street in Cork city, Michael John Francis O'Donovan would become clearly the most famous short story writer that Ireland has ever had. He lived an impoverished lonely childhood; which is best illustrated in his autobiography *An Only Child* (1961), in which O'Connor describes his life growing up in Cork city. Frank rarely got on with his father who was a violent alcoholic; compared to the relationship he had with his mother with whom he was very close. He attended St Patrick's National School Cork city and later the North Monastery Christian Brothers' School, which he left in 1917 in order to work and provide for his parents.

As well as being an Irish and English speaker he was a self taught linguist of German and French. He was passionately patriotic, which can be seen in many of his writings and at the age of 15 joined the

1st Cork Brigade of the Irish Volunteers. Frank fought in the War of Independence and then in the Civil War, taking the Anti-Treaty side. It was at this point that he began to publish his first poems through a republican newspaper.

After the Civil War, he became a teacher and librarian, the latter being his profession from 1925 to 1938. His first collection of short stories *Guests of the Nation* was published in 1931 and gives further evidence of his nationalist views. His short stories are numerous and his other writings include novels, plays, and poetry. He chose the pseudonym 'Frank O'Connor' for writing, which included his mother's maiden name as well as his confirmation name. His most notable works, as well as those listed above include *Bones of Contention* (1936) and *The Big Fellow* (1937), a biography on the life of Michael Collins from 1916 to his death in 1922. Although O'Connor served on the Anti-Treaty side during the Civil War, he wrote about Collins with some admiration:

> *'...the humorous, vital, tense, impatient figure which shoots through the pages of contemporary history as it shot through the streets of Dublin with a cry of anguish for 'all the hours we waste asleep'. People were already growing accustomed to his ways; the warning thump of his feet on the stairs as he took them six at a time, the crash of the door and the searching look, and that magnetic power of revivifying the stalest air.'*

He was appointed Managing Director of the Abbey Theatre in 1937, but was forced to resign in 1939 after the death of W.B. Yeats. His second novel,*Dutch Interior* (1940), was banned under Irish censorship as indecent. Some of his translations from Gaelic to English were also banned but for some reason the Irish copies were freely available. He later used the pen name 'Ben Mayo' to avoid attention from his more controversial work.

In 1938, he married his first wife, Evelyn Bowen, a Welsh actress, the couple later having three children. In 1951, his short stories,

Travellers Samples was published and subsequently banned. O'Connor left Ireland to lecture at Harvard University in the United States. He divorced Evelyn in 1952 and the following year married an American woman named Harriet Rich.

The couple lived both in Ireland and in America, but while teaching at Stanford University in 1961, O'Connor suffered a stroke and the couple returned to Ireland for good. He received an Honorary Doctorate from Trinity College Dublin in 1962 for his radio program 'Interior Voices' and went on to lecture at the college in 1964. He continued with his writing right up until his death at home in William Place, Dublin city on the 10th of March 1966. The second part of his autobiography *My Father's Son* was posthumously published in 1968.

Frank O'Connor is buried in the centre of St Patrick's section, just off the main drive. The graveside oration was delivered by the poet and playwright Brendan Kennelly. This grave has three different sized rectangular limestone tablets which include his name and the following words from his friend W.B. Yeats, inscribed deeply into the stone.

'I pray that I, all foliage gone, may shoot into my joy'

Brian O'Nolan - Writer / Brian Ó Nuallain / Flann O'Brien / Myles na gGopaleen

In the list of Ireland's greatest writers, you will most certainly find the name Flann O'Brien. His real name was Brian O'Nolan and he was born in Strabane, Co Tyrone on the 5th of October 1911. O'Nolan's father, Michael worked with the Department of Customs and Excise and the family regularly moved to where ever his work took him. Michael was also a part time teacher and insisted on his children being educated at home and also that they only speak Irish within the household. By the time he was aged 12 the family settled in Blackrock Co Dublin, with Brian starting school at Synge Street Christian Brothers in the city. He later attended Blackrock College and then went on to study languages

Memorial on the grave of Brian O'Nolan (Brian Ó Nuallain / Flann O'Brien / Myles na gGopaleen) and members of his family.

at UCD in 1929, a delight to O'Nolan as his favourite writer James Joyce had also studied there. It was in college that he wrote satirical and humorous articles for student journals. He graduated in 1932 with a B.A. in Irish, German, and English, and an M.A. in Celtic Studies in 1935, spending a year in Germany as part of the Language Degree. On leaving college O'Nolan followed his father into the Civil Service and held various governmental positions over the next 18 years of service. In December 1948, Brian married his fiancée Evelyn McDonnell.

As with the start of his articles in college, he would continue with his own brand of satirical writing that would last throughout his career. He was a journalist, a playwright, a fictional novelist of five books, and would muster up the occasional poem. One such poem 'The Workman's Friend' includes the following phrase:

'A pint of plain is your only man'

His first book published in 1939. *At Swim-Two-Birds* was written under this most used pen name 'Flann O'Brien' and would be regarded as his finest work. *An Béal Bocht* (1941) was written in Gaelic and later translated into English as *The Poor Mouth* in 1973. He penned *The Third Policeman* in 1940, but this wasn't published until 1967, a year after his death. *The Hard Life* was printed in 1961 and centres on realities of Irish social life. He even tried the patience of the Irish censorship board, going as far as naming one of its characters 'Father Fahrt', a swipe at the Catholic churches control on Irish censorship. His final novel, *The Dalkey Archive* (1965) features a character called 'De Selby' an insane scientist who tries to remove all the air from the earth's atmosphere.

O'Nolan found another outlet for his humour when he began writing his satirical column in the *Irish Times,* 'Cruiskeen Lawn' in 1940 and continued with this widely read column until his death in 1966. This was a bi-lingual column that he wrote under the pseudonym, 'Myles na gGopaleen' and resulted in three publications of its excerpts. *The Best of*

Myles is a collection of his best material from Cruiskeen Lawn. *At War*, was also a collection from the war years 1940–45 and *Further Cuttings from Cruiskeen Lawn* was printed after his death in 1968. Through Cruiskeen Lawn, O'Nolan chose to make fun and even attack those in government and Irish society whose point of view he did not share. The following is a line from the column in which O'Nolan states:

> *'The majority of the members of the Irish parliament are professional politicians, in the sense that otherwise they would not be given jobs minding mice at crossroads.'*

He occasionally wrote in a number of dramas for Radio Telefís Éireann (RTE) and also manuscript stage plays that included *Faustus Kelly* and *The Boy from Ballytearim*. *Faustus Kelly* was again mockingly directed at politics and was produced in the Abbey Theatre in 1947.

O'Nolan, like many Irish writers, had a fondness for public houses and the partaking of the odd drink. It was this fondness that would ultimately lead to his early demise. He died at the age of 54 on the 1st of April 1966, oddly enough April Fools Day.

Brian O'Nolan was buried beside his mother and father in a grave located directly in front of the Republican Plot in the West section. The headstone is made of granite and is uniquely carved to represent a Celtic cross with the individual inscriptions in Gaelic. It also states here that his wife Evelyn, who died in 1995, is buried with him now.

Noel Purcell – Actor / Comedian / Singer

The actor Noel Purcell was born in Dublin on the 23rd of December 1900. He was educated at Synge Street CBS and, at the age of 12, began work as a time caller for performers at the Gaiety Theatre, and sometimes as the hind legs of a donkey. By the age of 16, Noel began a 7 year apprenticeship as a joiner. But it was the theatre where Purcell most loved to be and where he cut his teeth as an actor, appearing in many stage plays and pantomimes, and some most memorably as a

'Dame'. His tall 6'4' frame, fully clad in flowing dress, makeup, and bonnet would be a pantomime in itself. He also continued with theatre up until 1984 with various rolls in performances from *Juno and the Paycock* to *Joseph and the Amazing Technicolor Dreamcoat.*

He played Dame Longshanks in *Little Red Riding Hood* in 1929 along side 12 year old Eileen Marmion, who played the Little Red Riding Hood. A number of years later, the two would meet after a long absence and fall in love as adults. Despite the 17 year age difference, Noel proposed to Eileen on Grafton Street in 1940. She accepted and the couple would spend the rest of their lives together and have a family of four sons. Noel got a great kick out of telling friends 'Eileen waited for me to grow up'.

His film career began in 1926 when he played the part of a Garda Sergeant in the silent movie *Blarney*, but it wasn't until 1947 that he would be first cast as Daniel McGinty in *Captain Boycott*. He played many TV and film roles throughout the years, most of which were as a supporting actor. Because of his large white beard, Noel was an ideal character to appear in nautical films; he could be best described as a skinny Santa Claus look-alike. The most notable of these seafaring flicks are *The Blue Lagoon* (1949), *The Crimson Pirate* (1952), and *Mutiny on the Bounty* (1962). Noel was also renowned for his ballad singing and he recorded amongst many of his favourite songs 'The Rare Old Times' and 'Dublin Saunter' which was composed for him by Leo Maguire.

He was a passionate Dub and very proud of his native city. In turn, the city was very proud of him. In June 1984 Noel was bestowed with the 'Freedom of Dublin City'. He humbly said after the award ceremony:

> *'It's a great honour. I never expected it. You really associate honours like this with physicists, doctors, and architects. Here am I an ex-carpenter, getting it. I am not worthy of it but I'm deeply, deeply honoured…'*

In February 1985, Noel accidentally fell at his home in Ballsbridge and was taken to the Adelaide hospital. Over the next few weeks his health slowly deteriorated, and it was on the morning of the 3rd of March 1985 that he quietly slipped away. On the morning of his funeral as the hearse arrived into the cemetery, his coffin was draped by a flag: not the Tricolour but a Dublin flag. His remains were interred in St Oliver's section. The grave is marked by a marble headstone and bears the following inscription:

'In loving memory of Noel Purcell,
Actor, Freeman of Dublin City,
died on the 3rd of March 1985, aged 84 Years'

William (Barry Fitzgerald) & Arthur Shields – Actor Brothers of Stage & Film

Actors William (better known as Barry Fitzgerald) and Arthur Shields are buried side by side, not far along from the funeral gate on the main drive. The brothers have separate headstones which are made of polished black granite with gold lettering, consisting of their names and the years each was born and died.

The elder of the two, William, was born in Dublin in March 1888. He was educated at Merchant Taylor's School and was later employed as a civil servant in 1911, having to use the stage name Barry Fitzgerald as an actor. He left the Civil Service in 1929 to become a full time performer.

William joined the Abbey Theatre and appeared in many plays throughout his career, most notably in Sean O'Casey's *Juno and the Paycock* and *The Plough and the Stars*. In 1930 he made his screen debut when *Juno and the Paycock* was turned into a film, directed by Alfred Hitchcock. He moved to the United States during the 30s, such was the demand for this little Irish character and he settled in California. He went on to appear in numerous other movies, most notably *The Long Voyage Home* (1940), starring John Wayne; *Going My Way* (1944), starring Bing Crosby; *The Story of Seabiscuit* (1949); and

The Quiet Man (1952), where he played 'Michaleen Oge Flynn', the old matchmaker between John Wayne and Maureen O'Hara. One of his best remembered sayings was as Michaleen in The Quiet Man when he turned to O'Hara and said...

'Is this a courting or a Donnybrook? Have the good manners not to hit the man until he's your husband and entitled to hit you back.'

In 1944, William was nominated for and received an Academy Oscar for Best Supporting Actor as 'Fr Fitzgibbon' in the film *Going My Way*. He was a comedian by nature and avid golfer by passion. After receiving his Oscar, William would tell friends he accidentally broke the head off it while practicing his golf swing.

Arthur was born in Dublin, eight years after William on the 15th of February 1896. Unlike his brother, Arthur generally played the more serious ecclesiastic roles in plays and films, as opposed to the lovable Irish rogue that William was more used to playing. In 1914 Arthur also began acting with the Abbey and became strongly influenced by nationalist plays like *The Plough and the Stars.* His nationalist views led him to join the Irish Volunteers and in 1916 he participated in the Easter Rising, chiefly based within the GPO. He was imprisoned in Frongoch internment camp Wales and was released later in the year and returned to acting at the Abbey.

In 1936, Arthur appeared in his first Hollywood movie, *The Plough and the Stars* as Padraig Pearse, a role he played alongside William and in which he was also the Assistant Director. The following year he took up full time residence in America. More films followed in the years ahead, such as *The Long Voyage Home* (1940)' with John Wayne; *How Green Was My Valley* (1941) with Maureen O'Hara; *National Velvet* (1944)' with Elizabeth Taylor and Mickey Rooney; *She Wore a Yellow Ribbon* (1949) and *The Quiet Man* (1952), in which he played the Rev Cyril 'Snuffy' Playfair.

As well his film roles, Arthur made guest appearances in various American TV series, amongst them *Perry Mason* and *Wagon Train,* and would spend the remainder of his life in the US.

On the 27th of April 1970, Arthur Shields died at his home in Santa Barbara California leaving behind his wife Laurie and two children. His remains were brought back to Ireland and interred beside those of his brother William who had died in Dublin on the 4th of January 1961. His coffin was draped in the Tri-colour as it entered the gates to the cemetery and an honour party from the Irish Army fired a volley of shots over his grave as a mark of respect. Ernest Blythe wrote in the Irish Times soon after his death

> *'...Arthur Shields did so well across the Atlantic that there was no question of a return to Ireland. But the fact that he is to be buried here like his brother shows that the fire which burned in him in 1916 was never quenched.'*

Davy Stephens – Newsagent & local Dún Laoghaire character

Most of those buried in Dean's Grange Cemetery are scarcely known outside of their own family, friends, or locality, but occasionally you come across names that are a little special. On some old postcards of Dún Laoghaire, you will find a peculiar little character selling newspapers. His name is Davy Stephens, a local newsagent that sold papers from under his arm on the steps of the train station and to passengers, coming and going from the ferry at Carlisle Pier. Stephens started selling papers at the age of 6 in order to provide for his mother and sisters, after his father died at a young age. He continued this profession and was able to open his own newsagents on Upper Georges Street in Dún Laoghaire. The character of Stephens would best be described as comical, witty, and chatty and not surprisingly, he wrote a book about his good self. He claimed to have met people coming off the Mail Boat from kings to paupers and to have treated them all with

Davy Stephens, as he appeared on postcards

the same jovial manner. His wit is best described in a passage from *The Life and Times of Davy Stephens,* when he was addressed by the Chief Secretary for Ireland one morning:

> *'Good morning Davy.*
> *Good Morning Sir.*
> *Any news this morning, Davy?*
> *Yes Sir, all under my arm here.'*

He became such a well known figure that he was commissioned to appear on postcards. In the cards, Stephens can be seen wearing a trilby hat and large black overcoat and sporting a very noticeable moustache that seemed to add to his sharp expression and overall rugged appearance. James Joyce, who was a frequent client of Stephens, immortalised him in his novel *Ulysses.*

> *'The door of Ruttledge's office creaked again. Davy Stephens, minute in a large capecoat, a small felt hat crowning his ringlets, passed out with a roll of papers under his cape, a king's courier.'*

He never missed a Derby race meeting in his adult life and as he did not drink nor smoke, the odd flutter on the horses was his only bad habit. On the 10th of September 1925, 'The King of the Irish Newsagents' as he was known, died at the age of 83. Davy's remains were buried two days later in the West section of the cemetery. The grave is located 15 plots past the Consecration Cross and two graves into the left. The headstone is of a Celtic cross design and is made of granite.

(Sir) Edward Sullivan - Lord Chancellor of Ireland / Politician

Edward Sullivan was born in Mallow, Co Cork on the 10th of July 1822. His father was a wealthy local merchant, who ensured his son would have the best education going, a decision which led to his son's great success. He was schooled locally before his enrolment into the Endowed School in Midleton. He entered Dublin's Trinity College in

1841 where he was well renowned for his debating abilities; he later received a gold medal for oratory.

After graduating with a B.A. in 1845 Sullivan studied at the Chambers London until 1848, when he was called to the Irish Bar. Although he was Protestant, in 1850 Sullivan married his fiancée Elizabeth 'Bessie' Bailey, a Catholic from Passage West Co Cork. The couple later went on to have five children.

The year 1858 saw the start of his progressive judicial career, with an appointment as a 'Queens Council' and then later in 1860 becoming an adviser to the Attorney General. He was again promoted the following year and in 1865 became the 'Solicitor General for Ireland' which only lasted a year before the Liberal Party were forced into opposition government. It was in his latter role as Solicitor General that Sullivan took charge in suppressing the Fenian Rising, resulting in the imprisonment and deportation of many Irishmen to Australia. That same year he was elected as a Liberal Party M.P. in Cork, a position he held for five years. When the Party won power again in 1868, Prime Minister William Gladstone appointed Sullivan, 'Attorney General for Ireland'. Sullivan's acute knowledge of his homeland and his debating abilities were used by Gladstone to endorse the 'Church Disestablishment Act' in the House of Commons in 1869. His services to the party were recognised in 1870, when he retired from parliament to take up the position of 'Master of the Rolls of Ireland'. He held this post for 13 years, while also maintaining his membership of the government's Privy Council, advising Gladstone on many issues. In 1881 the decision to arrest Charles Stewart Parnell was attributed to advice given by Sullivan. He was made a 'Baronet' in December 1881 becoming Sir Edward Sullivan of Garryduff Co Cork.

In 1883 Sir Edward Sullivan was appointed 'Lord High Chancellor of Ireland', the highest judicial office in the country. During his time as Chancellor he would again be called on to deal with nationalist issues, this time culminating in the suppression of the 'Invincibles'. The group had gained notoriety the previous year after they killed the nephew of Prime Minster William Gladstone in the Phoenix Park.

Sullivan died suddenly in his home at Fitzwilliam Place Dublin on the 13th of April 1885 while still Lord Chancellor. His remains were interred in a grave behind the Protestant Chapel, on which now stands one of the most impressive Celtic cross's in the cemetery. It is made of limestone and rises roughly 10 feet high from the base on which lies his inscription. The front of the cross is covered in intricate carvings consisting of hounds and birds feeding from grape vines and serpents with their tails interweaving and tracing back towards their mouths. The cross also shows a number of standard Celtic knots and other interweaving designs, especially at the top of the cross and circle.

(Capt) James Vaughan - Indian Rising (Indian Mutiny) & Lucknow relief force

If you walk past the Catholic chapel towards St Patrick's section, you will notice directly in front of you, at the junction, a very impressive monument to James Vaughan. This is the burial plot of James Vaughan, an ex-captain of the Royal Navy, and his family, who resided at Stradbrook Hall not far from the cemetery. The memorial consists of three tombs surrounded by link chains and posts. The large marble headstone consists of a ships anchor and chain resting against a cross with what appears to be a flag to the rear and a sword to the front. There is also a large rectangular base altar, which is inscribed with the following epitaph:

'Sacred to the memory of
Captain James Vaughan R.N – C.B.
who departed this life 29th April 1873, aged 44 years.
He entered the Royal Navy in the year 1841 on board HMS 'Scout'
and was present at the operations on the River Plate.
As Lieutenant, he served in the Baltic and Black Seas during the years
1854-6 and in the latter, on board HMS Britannia, took part in the

attack on the batteries of Sebastopol.In 1857 he joined
HMS Shannon Captain Sir William Peel V.C. – K.C.B.,
as senior Lieutenant and proceeded to India, during the Mutiny
he served as second in command of the Naval Brigade under that
officer and on his death from small pox assumed the sole command.
He advanced to the relief of Lucknow and there distinguished
himself by his coolness and daring in taking his guns within a few
yards of the walls and breaching them for the storming party.
For his services with the brigade he was promoted to the rank of
Commander, was awarded the Companionship of the Bath and on
his arrival in England, was further advanced to the rank of captain.
As well as being a thorough sailor, he was an accomplished
and gallant officer, an affectionate and devoted husband,
a warm and sincere friend and died beloved
and regretted by all who knew him.
This monument is erected by his widow,
Margaret Vaughan.'

The following is a brief overview of Vaughan's role in the Indian Rising:

James William Vaughan was a Lieutenant and then Commander on board HMS *Shannon* (under Captain William Peel) during the years 1857/58. The *Shannon* was a 51-gun steam frigate, the largest afloat at the time of her launch, and would have well in excess of 550 officers and men aboard. The ship was commissioned by Peel in September 1856 and destined for the China Seas.

On the ships arrival in Hong Kong the captain was to learn of the rising by Sepoy soldiers in India and they set sail again, this time for Calcutta. The Shannon was dispatched to India in order to assist in the suppression of the rising and after arriving at the mouth of Ganges in August 1857 Peel and his men were to join the Lucknow relief force. The sailors had to make their way up river and across land towards

Lucknow with their guns in tow. This journey was by men who were normally accustomed to voyages across oceans by ship and not by land on foot. Also taking into account that many of cannons they took along had eight-inch diameter barrels and other 24-pounder guns, this was going to be a rough journey. This arsenal had to be pulled along by the sailors with oxen, which was no easy task in the dry and harsh terrain.

During an attempt that December to repair a suspension bridge at a river crossing over the Kali-Naddi, a group under the command of Vaughan were fired upon by Sepoy native fighters and they quickly crossed the river with three of their guns. On reaching the far side they held back a body of Cavalry and destroyed the native's gun which was firing on them earlier from the small village of Khudaganj. Vaughan was able to totally destroy the gun position with five shots. The following month Vaughan was promoted to Commander and by that March the company reached Lucknow. Mid-March saw a brigade under the command of Vaughan again taking part in another major incident. His group blew open one of the gates to the courts of the Kaisarbagh which was the main Sepoy strong hold in Lucknow. By the end of the month the British force had taken control of the city. The brigade handed over to the new garrison, six of their eight-inch guns which they had brought up from the *Shannon*. The guns were then placed in the small battlement there and the word 'Shannon' was engraved into each carriage.

The sailors again turned towards Calcutta and didn't reach their ship until the end of August. On the 15th of September 1858 the Shannon set sail for home.

Commander Vaughan received the C.B. (Companionship of the Bath), an honour which was never before awarded to an officer of such low rank and also received the 'Relief of Lucknow clasp'. On the 8th of February 1859 Vaughan was posted as a captain of the Royal Navy and would hold this position until his retirement from the force on the 1st of April 1870.

Ernest Walton - Nobel Prize in Physics

Ernest Thomas Sinton Walton was born in Strandside South, Dungarven Co Waterford on the 6th of October 1903. The son of a Methodist minister, he attended schools in counties Down and Tyrone as his father moved between different towns. At the age of 12, he was enrolled by his father in the Methodist College, Belfast, and in 1922 he attended to studies in Trinity College Dublin. Ernest studied mathematics and science/physics and in 1926 graduated with first class honours. The following year he achieved his masters degree in science and was awarded a research scholarship to Cambridge University. He received his PhD from Cambridge by 1931 and returned to Trinity College in 1934 as a fellow.

It was also in this year that he married Freda Wilson, the daughter of a Methodist Minster and also a former pupil of the Methodist College Belfast, the couple would eventually have five children.

While at Cambridge, Walton began studying hydrodynamics and nuclear physics and met his friend and colleague John Cockcroft. While working together Walton and Cockcroft would ultimately split the nucleus of a lithium atom through artificial means. The two had created Helium Nuclei by splitting the atom using high voltages. It was for this work that they received the 'Hughes Medal' from the Royal Society, the UK's National Science Academy in 1938. But it was in 1951 that the two received their greatest award. The Nobel Foundation awarded Ernest Walton and John Cockcroft the highly regarded 'Nobel Prize in Physics'.

Ernest continued to lecture at Trinity College where his ability to instruct and advise his students was considered exceptional, as he had the ability to present complicated matters in an easy to understand technique. He was made a senior fellow of Trinity in 1960 and by 1974 retired from the college aged 71. Walton had a long and valuable retirement receiving a list of honorary degrees and fellowships for many years.

Ernest Walton died in hospital in Belfast on the 25th of June 1995 at the age of 91. His remains were conveyed to Dublin and laid to rest beside those of his wife Freda in Dean's Grange Cemetery. The grave which lies just inside the main gate in St Nessan's, has a small polished granite plaque. The words 'Nobel Laureate' are inscribed underneath his name.

The following is part of the speech Walton gave at the Nobel banquet in Stockholm, December 1951:

> *'I wish to thank the Royal Swedish Academy of Sciences very sincerely for the great honour they have done me. It is an honour so great that even yet it is difficult for me to believe that it is true. I have tried to think of any honour which I would prefer to this one and I have failed to do so.'*

Joseph Edward Woodall - Victoria Cross Recipient

There is a rich military history within the town land of Dún Laoghaire and this is no more in evidence than in this cemetery. A walk through the South and South-West sections will open the visitor's eyes to the graves of those who served in British regiments and in some cases by generations of the same family. But it is in St Patrick's section where the remains of the most honoured of all these British soldiers, Joseph Woodall is buried.

Joseph Edward Woodall

Woodall was born in Salford Manchester on the 1st of June 1896. He joined the British Army and served with the 1st Battalion Rifle Brigade (Prince Consort's Own) during the First World War. It was while serving at La Pennerie France on the 22nd of April 1918 that

Woodall carried out a heroic act that would lead to him being awarded the Victoria Cross, the highest honour that can be awarded to a member of the British or Commonwealth forces.

Woodall's unit was advancing at La Pennerie when they came under fire from an enemy machine gun which had managed to pin the unit down. On his own, Lance-Sergeant Woodall left his men and rushed the enemy position, capturing the gun and its eight German soldiers. Later he and a number of his men captured a further 30 prisoners when they overpowered another position at a farmhouse, again while under heavy fire. It was not long afterwards that his Officer Commanding was killed, leaving Woodall to take full command of the unit, a task it was reported he carried out with such professionalism and courage, and with the full respect of his unit. All this was at a time when Woodall was only 21 years old and a Non-Commissioned Officer.

Joseph Woodall was promoted to the rank of captain before eventually leaving the army in 1921. He later moved to Ireland, settling with a family named King in the village of Sandycove, to the East of Dún Laoghaire. Joseph suffered from spells of fits and fainting and was undergoing treatment to help deal with these ailments. The fits were as a result of his time served during the war and from which he never fully recovered. While alone in his room one day Joseph collapsed and fell against an electric fire. It was some time before a member of the King family heard moans coming from his room and found Joseph lying on the floor suffering from serious burns. He was rushed to St Michael's Hospital but died there from his injuries on the 2nd of January 1962.

There is very little known about Joseph and his life up until his death at the age of 64 and it seems he kept a low key existence. His remains were interred in the lower end of the St Patrick's section but there is no mention of Joseph on the 'King' headstone which marks the grave.

Bibliography

1916 Rebellion Handbook, The Mourne River Press 1998

The Irish Times Book of the 1916 Rising, Shane Hegarty & Fintan O'Toole 2006

The Easter Rebellion, Max Caulfield 1995

Survivors, Related to: Uinseann MacEoin 1980

The Last Post 3rd Edition 1916 – 1985, National Graves Association 1985

The Royal Navy, Clowes, William Laird 1903

Journal of Lieutenant E. Hope Verney, R.N, Saunders and Otley. W.H.G. Kingston

Who's Who, Padraic O'Farrell 1997

Three Villages, Donal Foley 1977

The Women of the Abbey Theatre 1897-1925, Robin Jackson Boisseau 2004

The Burning of the Custom House in Dublin 1921, Sean O'Mahony 2000

Book Series Les Prix Nobel / Nobel Lectures

Nobel Lectures Physics 1942-1962, Elsevier Publishing Company 1964

The Big Fellow, Frank O'Connor 1937

Derbyshire Lads at War: 1914 – 1918, John McGuiggan

Dean's Grange Cemetery, Vicky Cremin 1989

Dublin's Burial Grounds and Graveyards, Vivian Igoe 2002

Green Against Green, The Irish Civil War, Michael Hopkinson 1988

Mother of all the Behan's, Brian Behan 1984
Revolutionary Woman, Kathleen Clarke (Helen Litton) 1991
Blood on the Streets, Paul O'Brien 2008
Louie Bennett IWWU, John Murphy
Courageous Irish Women, John Gallagher
Noel Purcell a Biography, Philip Bryan 1992
Wreck & Rescue, John De Courey Ireland 1983
Lifeboats in Dublin Bay, John De Courey Ireland 1997
In the Mind's Eye, Dun Laoghaire Borough Heritage Society 1991
Dun Laoghaire Borough Historical Society, Dun Laoghaire *Journal No. 9* (2000), 13 (2004), 14 (2005)
Ireland in Quotes, Conor O'Clery 2000
Assassination, Rex Taylor 1961
Ulysses, James Joyce 1922
Torpedoed!, Philip Lecane 2005
Leinster Log, William Byrne & Philip Lecane October 2002
Death in the Irish Sea, Roy Stokes 1998
Vanity Fair Magazine & Supplement May 1910
An Assembly of Irish Surgeons, J.B. Lyons 1984
DLRCC, *Dean's Grange Cemetery Records 1864 - 2008*
A new Dictionary of Irish History from 1800, DJ Hickey & JE Doherty 2005
A Dictionary of Irish Biography, Henry Boylan 1998
The IRA, Tim Pat Coogan 1990
Free Noel Jenkinson Campaign Leaflet
The Book of Kells, described by Sir Edward Sullivan 1920
Dublins Fighting Story, Michael Chadwick 1949
Down Dublin Streets 1916, Éamonn MacThomáis 1965
The Squad, T. Ryle Dwyer 2005
A Dictionary of Irish Biography, Henry Boylan 1988

NEWSPAPERS:

The Bray Herald and Arklow Reporter, Palme Disaster 1881/2
Poblacht Na hEirean / War News, Civil War
Republican War Bulletin, Civil War
Evening Herald, Palme Disaster 1881/2
Insignia / The Evening Telegram Oct 1997, Philip Little
Irish Post, Aug 1980 Dunne & O'Sullivan
Freeman's Journal, various
The Irish Times, various
The Irish Independent, various
Illustrated London News, Nov & Dec 1881
The Kingstown Journal 1861/5
The Bray Gazette 1861/5

WEBSITES:

www.culturenorthernireland.org, Augustine Henry
www.universityscience.ie, Augustine Henry
www.themodernword.com, Brian O'Nolan
www.centerforbookculture.org, Brian O'Nolan
www.irishwarmemorials.ie, British War Graves
www.askaboutireland.ie, Davy Stephens
www.findagrave.com, Dermot Morgan
www.waterfordcountymuseum.org, Donal Foley
www.catholicireland.net, Edward Sullivan
www.understandingscience.ucc.ie, Ernest Walton
www.nndb.com, Frank O'Connor
www.bedfordstmartins.com, Frank O'Connor
www.ucc.ie, Frank O'Connor
www.wiu.edu, Frank O'Connor
www.rds.ie, Howard Grubb

www.universityscience.ie, Howard Grubb
www.legacyrecordings.com, John Count McCormack
www.mccormacksociety.Couk, John Count McCormack
www.victoriacross.org.uk, Joseph Edward Woodall
www.siptu.ie, Louie Bennett
www.imdb.com, various people
www.biographi.ca, Philip Francis Little
www.huntmuseum.com, Sybil Connolly
www.irishartsreview.com, Sybil Connolly
www.nationalarchives.ie, various people
www.answers.com, various people
en.wikipedia.org, various people
www.politics.ie, various people
www.pgil-eirdata.org, various people
www.dougmacaulay.com, William & Arthur Shields
www.graham.thewebtailor.Couk, Dunne & O'Sullivan
www.rampantscotland.com, John Boyd Dunlop
www.botanicgardens.ie, Augustine Henry
www.biographi.ca, Philip Francis Little
www.turlach.net, Donagh MacDonagh
www.iol.ie, Delia Murphy
www.catholicireland.net, Edward Sullivan
www.comedy-zone.net, Dermot Morgan
www.ulsterhistory.Couk, Joseph Campbell
www.familyhistory.ie, Sea Disasters & Various
http://nifg.Couk, James Dunne
www.shamrockrovers.ie, James Dunne
www.tcd.ie, various people

Index of Graves

NAME	SURNAME	PLOT	SECTION	LISTING	D.O.D.
Hector John	Atkinson	75 P	South-West	CWGC	1917-05-26
George Henderson	Baird	36 K2	South	CWGC	1919-11-09
John	Baker	89 I1	North	RLNI	1895-12-24
John	Bambrick	51 G4	North	Civil War	1922-07-01
Emily	Barlow	91 O1	South-West	Leinster	1918-10-10
Daniel	Barry	11 C3	West	CWGC	1917-11-03
John	Bartley	15 N2	South	RLNI	1895-12-24
Kathleen	Behan	19 H	St Kevin's	Notable	1984-04-27
Herbert	Bell	90 N1	South-West	CWGC	1918-07-29
Alan	Bell	71 G	South-West	Tan War	1920-03-26
Louie B	Bennett	62 I	South-West	Notable	1956-11-25
Christopher	Beresford	63 J3	North	CWGC	1919-08-07
Richard Irvine	Best	66 H	South-West	Notable	1959-09-25
Thomas Christopher	Blake	14 Z	St Ita's	CWGC	1945-09-30
JS	Blissett	85 T1	South-West	1916 CWGC	1916-04-26
William	Breen	74 C4	North	CWGC	1941-08-26

NAME	SURNAME	PLOT	SECTION	LISTING	D.O.D.
John	Brennan	10 P2	West	CWGC	1918-02-01
Andrew	Breslin	24 R	St Ita's	CWGC	1941-01-12
Montague Bernard	Browne	85 T1	South-West	1916 CWGC	1916-04-26
Francis Henry	Browning	27 U	South	1916	1916-04-26
Reginald Patrick	Buckley	40 S2	West	CWGC	1945-05-02
William	Burnell	Protestant Chapel	South-West	Overview	1926-10-10
William	Byrne	8 T2	West	CWGC	1940-11-21
Andrew	Byrne	25 U2	West	1916	1916-04-27
James	Byrne	11 Y	West	Notable	1913-11-01
Charles	Byrne	42 L	North	Solway	1881-11-17
Matthew	Campbell	17 K2	West	CWGC	1916-05-19
Joseph	Campbell	91 C	North	Notable	1944-06-06
Charles J	Canning	86 M1	South-West	CWGC	1918-10-16
Anastasia	Carey	31 K	North	Notable	1865-01-27
William	Carrick	25 V2	West	1916	Easter Week
James Joseph	Carroll	7A	West	1916	1916-04-28

NAME	SURNAME	PLOT	SECTION	LISTING	D.O.D.
James	Cash	41 J3	North	CWGC	1918-11-07
John	Cash	41 J3	North	CWGC	1919-02-21
Richard Archibald	Cathie	82 F1	South-West	CWGC	1918-03-20
Joseph	Clarke	25 U2	West	1916	Easter Week
John Daly	Clarke	39 Io	St Brigid's	Notable	1971-05-22
Kathleen	Clarke	38 Io	St Brigid's	Notable	1972-09-29
Mary Edith	Coleman	30 S2	South	Notable	1906-09-23
Michael	Connolly	12 M1	West	CWGC	1917-12-25
Christopher	Connolly	75 T3	North	CWGC	1919-11-21
Sybil	Connolly	37 A	St Itas	Notable	1998-05-06
Joseph	Connor	23 O1	West	CWGC	1917-02-25
Joseph D	Cope	17 A	South	Overview	1899-04-09
Joseph	Costello	25 V2	West	1916	1916-04-26
John A	Costello	120 M	St Patrick's	Notable	1976-01-05
Denis	Crimmins	50 H	West	CWGC	1920-02-21
Edward	Crowe	26 G4	North	RLNI	1895-12-24

NAME	SURNAME	PLOT	SECTION	LISTING	D.O.D.
Michael J	Cullen	6 B2	West	CWGC	1919-11-04
Andrew	Cunningham	36 T3	West	1916	1916-05-01
James Gerard (Rev)	Curran	1P / Holy Ghost Fathers	West	CWGC	1944-05-04
Frederick Christian	Dietrichsen	66 K2	South	1916 CWGC	1916-04-26
Henry	Doran	43 J	West	CWGC	1920-05-15
Edward	Dorins	95 A4	North	Tan War	1921-05-25
Herbert Richard	Dowse	14 P	St Nessan's	CWGC	1944-10-21
Daniel	Doyle	22 P4	West	CWGC	1918-10-12
Arthur	Doyle	30 N	West	CWGC	1919-02-14
John	Doyle	30 E1	West	1916	1916-05-01
John Boyd	Dunlop	73 D	South-West	Notable	1921-10-23
Hugh	Dunne	59 T3	North	CWGC	1915-01-27
James	Dunne	29 S1	St Ita's	Notable	1949-11-14
Reginald	Dunne	16 B / Rep Plot	West	Tan War	1922-08-10
William	Dunphy	88 H1	North	RLNI	1895-12-24

NAME	SURNAME	PLOT	SECTION	LISTING	D.O.D.
Thomas	Dunphy	88 I1	North	RNLI	1895-12-24
Mary	Dwyer	35 T3	West	1916	1916-05-04
John	Eager	3 G	St Fintan's	CWGC	1940-08-12
Charles Robert	Easton	20 N2	West	CWGC	1918-06-16
Elizabeth	Ellam	85 R	South-West	Leinster	1918-10-10
Private	Ellis	25 U2	West	1916 CWGC	1916-04-28
Alfred	Ellis	85 S1	South-West	1916 CWGC	1916-05-01
Peter	Ennis	25 V2	West	1916 CWGC	1916-04-25
Thomas Henry	Evans	76 S	South-West	CWGC	1918-06-06
Patrick	Farrell	71 D	St Mary's	CWGC	1944-05-30
James	Farrell	12 F	St Fintan's	CWGC	1944-09-21
Thomas L C	Farrell	24 F1	St Fintan's	CWGC	1945-06-08
Peter	Farrell	205 C	St Patrick's	Notable	1999-03-16
Kevin Finbarr	Fidgeon	72 H	St Mary's	CWGC	1941-11-24
Daniel Patrick	Finn	103 F1	North	CWGC	1918-04-30
James	Fitzpatrick	57 I	West	CWGC	1920-05-01

NAME	SURNAME	PLOT	SECTION	LISTING	D.O.D.
Michael William	Fitzpatrick	88 G3	North	CWGC	1945-03-24
John	Flynn	105 K	North	1916	Easter Week
Donal	Foley	46 J	St Anne's	Notable	1981-07-07
John	Gardiner Nutting	78 N	South-West	Notable	1918-02-18
Percy Gerald	Gilbert	35 U1	South	CWGC	1918-11-19
Ernest E	Glorney	75 Aa / Bb	South-West	CWGC	1916-10-25
Christina Sophie	Goodman	97 A	South	Leinster	1918-10-10
Peter	Graham	30 A3	West	Tan War	1921-05-15
Robert Kingston	Gray	12 M2	South	CWGC	1918-11-02
William	Gregg	34 S3	West	1916	1916-04-29
Howard (Sir)	Grubb	90 O	South-West	Notable	1931-09-16
Charles E	Harman	69 J	South-West	CWGC	1915-01-05
Peter	Harold	38 V	St Ita's	CWGC	1943-06-08
John Joseph	Healy	82 G1	North	Tan War	1921-02-12
Augustine	Henry	56 I4	North	Notable	1930-03-23
Christopher	Hickey	28 P3	West	1916	1916-04-29

NAME	SURNAME	PLOT	SECTION	LISTING	D.O.D.
Thomas	Hickey	28 P3	West	1916	1916-04-29
John	Hickie	43 N	West	Tan War	1920-12-14
Jeremiah	Hogan	6 A	West	1916	1916-04-28
Stanley	Hollinshead	15 H	St Nessan's	CWGC	1943-12-04
Joseph	Hudson	18 B / Rep Plot	West	Civil War	1922-08-12
Arthur Walter Patrick	Inman	61 N1	South-West	CWGC	1920-06-17
Arthur H	Jeffries	90 T1	South-West	Leinster	1918-10-10
John	Jenkins	19 A / Rep Plot	West	Tan War	1922-05-04
Noel	Jenkinson	3 K	St Mogue's	Notable	1976-10-09
William J V	Johns	96 P1	South-West	CWGC	1920-12-20
Dorothy May	Jones	24 W	South	Leinster	1918-10-10
John H C	Jones	5 W1	South	Civil War	1922-08-28
William	Joyce	38 W2	West	CWGC	1918-12-26
Peter	Judge	121 G	St Patrick's	Notable	1947-04-24
Eileen	Judge (Crowe)	121 G	St Patrick's	Notable	1978-05-08
John	Keely	70 Z3	North	1916	1916-04-25

NAME	SURNAME	PLOT	SECTION	LISTING	D.O.D.
Michael	Kelly	45 O1	North	CWGC	1916-08-05
Patrick	Kelly	40 H	West	CWGC	1919-11-23
James Joseph	Kelly	43 C1	West	CWGC	1941-02-14
Mary	Kelly	9 A2	West	1916	1916-04-30
Herbert Colles	Kennedy	61 O	South-West	CWGC	1918-10-15
James	Kennedy	20 Q	West	CWGC	1919-04-09
Charles	Kenny	5 R	West	CWGC	1918-02-17
Peter	Kenny	47 A1	North	Civil War	1922-08-20
John	Keynon	25 U2	West	1916	Easter Week
William	Lang	Special Memorial	South-West	1916 CWGC	1916-04-26
Martin	Lawlor	94 Q3	North	CWGC	1917-03-13
Robert Ernest	Lee	47 D1	South	Leinster	1918-10-10
Sean	Lemass	39 R	St Patrick's	Notable	1971-04-11
Richard	Lennon	90 E1	North	CWGC	1917-09-25
Philip Francis	Little	1 F2	North	Notable	1897-10-21
George C	Lugton	91 N1	South-West	CWGC	1918-10-10

NAME	SURNAME	PLOT	SECTION	LISTING	D.O.D.
Patrick	Lynch	28 U	West	CWGC	1918-05-16
John	Lynch	57 Z3	West	CWGC	1946-11-01
Thomas William	Lyster	45 M2	South	Notable	1922-12-12
Donagh	MacDonagh	137 Ao	North	Notable	1968-01-01
Thomas	Maher	22 E1	West	CWGC	1918-10-30
William	Maher	54 Y	St Nessan's	Notable	1953-06-11
Harry G	Manning	21 P2	South	Civil War	1922-11-13
Patrick M	Mannion	20 P2	North	Civil War	1922-09-17
Cyril John	Massy	71 V1	South-West	CWGC	1947-04-07
James Bernard	McCall	3 M	St Mary's	CWGC	1944-02-01
John (Count)	McCormack	120 E	St Patrick's	Notable	1945-09-16
Francis	McDonald	126 P	North	RLNI	1895-12-24
Joseph	McGrath	28 E	St Patrick's	Notable	1966-03-26
Margaret	McGuinness	92 T3	North	1916	1916-05-03
James	McIntosh	19 B / Rep Plot	West	Tan War	1921-06-22
Patrick	McIntyre	18 K2	West	1916	1916-04-26

NAME	SURNAME	PLOT	SECTION	LISTING	D.O.D.
Thomas Alexander	McLoughlin	71 X1	South-West	CWGC	1943-07-02
Jessie	McTaggart	83 Z	South-West	CWGC	1919-01-21
Alfred P	Miller	30 B2	West	CWGC	1920-06-24
Dermot	Morgan	106 R	St Patrick's	Notable	1998-03-01
John	Mulhern	49 L	West	1916 CWGC	1916-04-24
Joseph	Murphy	28 N1	North	CWGC	1916-01-07
Robert Anthony	Murphy	34 E4	North	CWGC	1947-01-02
Charles 'Rodney'	Murphy	17 B / Rep Plot	West	Civil War	1922-09-01
Edward	Murphy	86 I1	North	RLNI	1895-12-24
Thomas	Murphy	25 Q1	West	Tan War	1921-05-30
Delia	Murphy (Kiernan)	173 Io	St Brigid's	Notable	1971-02-12
Martin	Murray	23 XX	North	CWGC	1918-06-30
Edward 'Leo'	Murray	17 B / Rep Plot	West	Civil War	1922-09-01
Richard	O'Brien	29 K1	St Fintan's	CWGC	1945-08-27
Thomas	O'Byrne	41 A3	St Brigid's	1916	1964-12-15
Frank	O'Connor	80 N	St Patrick's	Notable	1966-03-10

NAME	SURNAME	PLOT	SECTION	LISTING	D.O.D.
Christopher	O'Flaherty	105 K	North	1916	Easter Week
Annie	O'Neill	96 N3	North	Tan War	1920-11-13
Brian	O'Nolan	20 A	West	Notable	1966-04-01
Joseph	O'Sullivan	16 B / Rep Plot	West	Tan War	1922-08-10
Patrick	O'Toole	6 J2	West	Leinster	1918-10-10
George	Parkinson	93 K	North	Solway	1881-11-16
James	Phoenix	20 Y2	West	CWGC	1918-04-27
Francis	Power	5 J3	North	Civil War	1922-11-02
Patrick	Power	53 I3	North	RLNI	1895-12-24
Patrick	Prendergast	127 R	North	CWGC	1920-05-27
Noel	Purcell	85 E	St Oliver's	Notable	1985-03-03
Gerard Philip	Regan	147 C	St Patrick's	CWGC	1944-12-07
Edward	Reilly	10 X2	West	CWGC	1917-05-13
James	Reilly	136 I	North	CWGC	1918-09-24
Arthur Ferdinand	Richards	103 A	North	CWGC	1940-11-24
David	Roberts	93 R1	South-West	CWGC	1919-03-25

NAME	SURNAME	PLOT	SECTION	LISTING	D.O.D.
Henry	Rooke	91 K1	South-West	CWGC	1918-10-08
Joseph	Ryan	34 G3	West	CWGC	1915-05-19
James	Ryan	87 H1	North	RLNI	1895-12-24
Michael	Saul	17 N	West	CWGC	1916-04-09
Robert	Saunders	11 T2	West	CWGC	1917-02-24
David Mansfield	Saunders	93 B	North	CWGC	1918-12-02
Charles	Saunders	85 S1	South-West	1916 CWGC	1916-04-28
Frances Elizabeth	Saunders	21 N2	south	Leinster	1918-10-10
George B	Saunders	20 H2	South	RLNI	1895-12-24
Francis	Saunders	21 H2	South	RLNI	1895-12-24
William	Scott	61 U	South-West	CWGC	1917-11-11
Edward	Shannon	87 I1	North	RLNI	1895-12-24
Joseph	Shargine	124 K	North	1916	Easter Week
William	Shields	58 A	St Nessan's	Notable	1961-01-04
Arthur	Shields	58 A	St Nessan's	Notable	1970-04-27
Alfred W	Smith	91 L1	South-West	CWGC	1918-10-09

NAME	SURNAME	PLOT	SECTION	LISTING	D.O.D.
William John	Smith	11 P4	West	Leinster	1918-10-10
Michael J	Smyth	48 S	West	Tan War	1921-05-29
Patrick	Smyth	14 N1	North	Civil War	1922-07-07
John Joseph	Stephens	17 B / Rep Plot	West	Civil War	1922-09-02
David (Davy)	Stephens	2 T	West	Notable	1925-09-10
Edward G	Stevens	92 N1	South-West	CWGC	1918-10-26
Bridget	Stewart	25 N3	West	1916	1916-04-28
Edward (Sir)	Sullivan	6 V	South	Notable	1885-04-13
George	Synnot	96 R	South-West	1916	1916-04-30
Joseph V	Tierney	109 H1	North	CWGC	1916-01-05
Ernest G	Tozer	91 S1	South-West	CWGC	1918-10-20
Michael	Tyrell	56 G4	North	CWGC	1918-11-10
Henry	Tyrrell	92 K1	North	Leinster	1918-10-10
Henry	Underhill	16 N2	South	RLNI	1895-12-24
James William (Capt)	Vaughan	36 B	North	Notable	1873-04-29
Peter P	Walsh	20 A1	St Ita's	CWGC	1943-07-10

NAME	SURNAME	PLOT	SECTION	LISTING	D.O.D.
Kate	Walsh	124 K	North	1916	Easter Week
Ernest T S	Walton	90 A	St Nessan's	Notable	1995-06-25
Maud Elizabeth	Ward	83 Q	South-West	Leinster	1918-10-10
Richard	Waters	75 Q	South-West	1916	1916-04-25
Samuel	Webb	47 C1	West	Civil War	1922-11-13
Sean	Wheeler	11 K2	West	CWGC	1941-07-13
William I De C	Wheeler	34 C	St Nessan's	CWGC	1943-09-11
William	Williams	91 P1	South-West	CWGC	1918-10-26
Alexander	Williams	17 N2	South	RLNI	1895-12-24
Henry	Williams	17 N2	South	RLNI	1895-12-24
Joseph Edward	Woodall	173 H	St Patrick's	Notable	1962-01-02
Christopher	Woodcock	124 K	North	1916	Easter Week
Huge Boyd	Wray	19 M	South	Overview	1873-02-23
Walter	Wright	Special Memorial	South-West	CWGC	1918-10-19
John S	Young	34 Q2	South	CWGC	1919-05-06